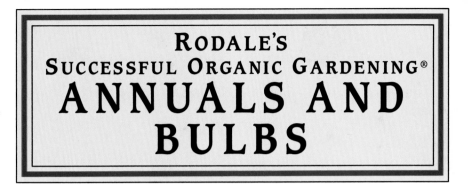

RODALE'S
SUCCESSFUL ORGANIC GARDENING®
ANNUALS AND BULBS

RODALE'S
SUCCESSFUL ORGANIC GARDENING®
ANNUALS AND BULBS

TEXT BY ROB PROCTOR

"GUIDE TO ANNUALS" AND "GUIDE TO BULBS" BY NANCY J. ONDRA

Rodale Press, Emmaus, Pennsylvania

Our Mission

We publish books that empower people's lives.

RODALE BOOKS

Library of Congress Cataloging-in-Publication Data

Proctor, Rob.
    Annuals and bulbs / text by Rob Proctor ; plant-by-plant guides by Nancy J. Ondra.
       p.   cm. — (Rodale's successful organic gardening)
    Includes index.
    ISBN 0–87596–669–1 (hardcover). — ISBN 0–87596–670–5 (paperback)
    1. Annuals (Plants). 2. Bulbs. 3. Organic gardening. I. Ondra, Nancy J. II. Title. III. Series.
    SB422.P77 1995
    635.9'312—dc20   95–13796

Printed in the United States of America on acid-free ∞, recycled paper ♻

Rodale Press Staff:
    Editorial Director, Home and Garden Books: Margaret Lydic Balitas
    Editor: Nancy J. Ondra
    Copy Editor: Carolyn R. Mandarano
    Editor-in-Chief: William Gottlieb

Produced for Rodale Press by Weldon Russell Pty Ltd
107 Union Street, North Sydney NSW 2060, Australia
a member of the Weldon International Group of Companies

    Chief Executive: Elaine Russell
    Managing Editor: Ariana Klepac
    Editorial Assistant: Cassandra Sheridan
    Horticultural Consultant: Cheryl Maddocks
    Copy Editor: Yani Silvana
    Designer: Honor Morton
    Picture Researcher: Elizabeth Connolly
    Illustrators: Tony Britt-Lewis, Barbara Rodanska, Jan Smith, Kathie Smith
    Indexer: Michael Wyatt
    Production Manager: Dianne Leddy

A KEVIN WELDON PRODUCTION

Distributed in the book trade by St. Martin's Press

2 4 6 8 10 9 7 5 3   hardcover
2 4 6 8 10 9 7 5 3 1   paperback

Opposite: *Tulipa* 'Monte Carlo' and *Muscari armeniacum*
Half title: *Papaver rhoeas* and *Centaurea cyanus*
Opposite title page: *Colchicum speciosum*
Title page: *Helianthus annuus*
Opposite contents: *Tulipa* hybrid and *Bellis perennis*
Contents: *Dahlia* hybrid (top left), *Mimulus* x *hybridus* (bottom left)

CONTENTS

INTRODUCTION

Annuals and bulbs are among the greatest bargains in the gardening world. For the price of one container-grown perennial, you can buy enough annual seeds to fill an entire garden bed (and then save the seeds from those plants to grow more each season!). Or you could invest in a dozen daffodil bulbs or several dozen crocus corms, and end up with hundreds of plants in a few years. It's hard to beat that kind of return on such a minimal investment.

Of course, gardening with annuals and bulbs isn't just about saving money. It's also about beautifying the landscape around your home with color and fragrance. From the first dainty crocuses in early spring to the bold, brightly colored rosettes of ornamental cabbage in late fall, annuals and bulbs provide loads of colorful blooms to your yard for nearly three-quarters of the year (or longer in mild-winter areas). And if that isn't enough, you can even bring some annuals and bulbs indoors for winter bloom!

Annuals and bulbs fit into any size or style of garden, from formal beds and borders to casual cottage gardens. Include annuals and bulbs in containers to create living bouquets that enliven outdoor living areas, such as patios, terraces, balconies, and porches. Grow these plants in a cutting garden to have a steady supply of fresh flowers for indoor arrangements. Turn a low-maintenance area into an eye-catching landscape feature with naturalized bulbs or an annual meadow garden. Try tall annuals and annual vines for quick shade or privacy, choose particular flower and foliage colors to create color theme gardens, or grow scented types to add an extra element of pleasure to your beautiful plantings.

If you're a beginning gardener, you'll appreciate how easy annuals and bulbs are to grow and how dependably they bloom. As you gain experience, you'll enjoy mixing them with perennials, groundcovers, grasses, shrubs, and other plants to create eye-catching combinations. Whatever your interest, *Rodale's Successful Organic Gardening: Annuals and Bulbs* will show you the way to creating gorgeous gardens with these versatile, easy-care plants.

Dependable and versatile, annuals and bulbs are an indispensable part of flower beds and borders. You can enjoy their beautiful blooms from early spring well into fall—even year-round in mild climates!

HOW TO USE THIS BOOK

Creating a successful garden depends on two factors—understanding the growing conditions your yard has to offer and choosing plants that will thrive there. Once you've matched the right plants to the right site, you're well on your way to having a naturally healthy and beautiful landscape. *Rodale's Successful Organic Gardening: Annuals and Bulbs* will guide you through the whole process of planning and planting a fabulous flower garden, from learning about your site and picking the best plants to creating easy-care plantings for color, fragrance, cut flowers, and more.

The garden-making process begins with understanding the plants that you're growing and what they need. "Gardening with Annuals and Bulbs," starting on page 12, will tell what you need to know about the different kinds of annuals and bulbs and the many ways you can incorporate them into your yard. You'll also learn how to identify your site's growing conditions—such as the amount of light and the type of soil—and how to choose plants that are best suited to those conditions. Plus, you'll find tips for putting compatible plants together to create simple but stunning combinations.

"Annuals in Your Garden," starting on page 28, goes into detail about the wonderful ways you can add annuals to your yard. Flower beds and borders are among the most popular ways to display annual flowers. But you can also use your creativity to group annuals for a particular purpose. Growing them in container gardens, for instance, is a fun and easy way to add color to spots where it isn't practical to have an in-the-ground garden. Bushy, easy-to-grow annuals are also useful for filling in gaps around new permanent plantings, such as perennial borders, foundation plantings, and groundcover patches.

If you're looking for a quick screen for shade or privacy,

"Annuals in Your Garden" includes suggestions of tall annuals or annual vines to try. You'll also learn about grouping annuals into color-theme gardens and growing cutting gardens for fresh and dried flowers. If you're fond of fragrance, you may choose to plan your gardens around scented annuals. Or, if cooking is one of your hobbies, consider growing a garden that contains annual herbs. You'll be amazed at the many wonderful ways flowering and foliage annuals can blend into just about any planting area your yard has to offer.

When you've decided which plants you want to grow and know where you want them to go, you're ready for "Growing Annuals," starting on page 42. Here's where you'll learn the down-and-dirty details of growing annuals from seed, buying healthy transplants, and getting your plants into the ground. You'll also find all the basics on caring for established annuals, including safe and effective techniques for coping with any pest or disease problems that show up.

Flowers that grow from bulbs and similar structures are as versatile in your landscape as annuals. "Bulbs in Your Garden," starting on page 104, is full of exciting and inspiring ideas for adding garden interest from spring through fall. You'll also find out how to "force" bulbs for winter bloom indoors and how to incorporate bulbs into beds, borders, and container plantings. Learn the tricks to "naturalizing" bulbs for masses of bloom in low-maintenance areas, and discover which bulbs are best for fresh cut-flower arrangements.

"Growing Bulbs," starting on page 124, is your source for the basics of raising beautiful bulbs, from buying and planting to caring for the plants through the year. You'll also find information on propagation techniques you can use to increase your stock of bulbs each year.

Plant-by-plant Guides

Picking out the plants you want to grow is one of the most fun parts of gardening with annuals and bulbs. To help you choose, this book includes two encyclopedia sections: the "Guide to Annuals," starting on page 58 and the "Guide to Bulbs," starting on page 138. Plants in both encyclopedia sections are arranged in alphabetical order by the botanical name. When you're interested in a particular plant, you can look it up in the appropriate guide. (If you aren't sure of the botanical name, simply look up the common name in the index, and it will refer you to the right place.) Or you could just skim through the guides and look at the pictures, then read about the plants that interest you.

Each entry gives all the basics you need to grow each plant successfully. You'll find a description and height and spread information in every entry, so you'll know how big the plant grows, what it looks like, and what color it is. You'll also find growing tips, as well as suggested landscape uses to give you ideas on how to site each plant most effectively in your garden. The diagram below is a sample of one of these practical pages.

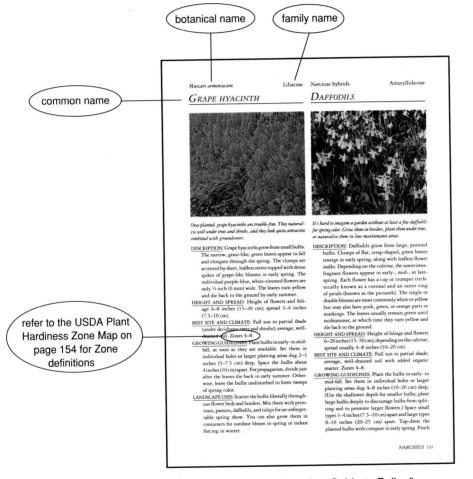

Sample page from the "Guide to Bulbs."

GARDENING WITH
ANNUALS AND BULBS

One of the great joys of gardening comes from experimenting with different plants. Two groups of plants—annuals and bulbs—offer particularly exciting opportunities for creative gardeners. If you're a beginner, you'll be gratified by the success you'll have with many easy annuals and bulbs. As you gain experience in flower gardening, you'll enjoy mixing all kinds of annuals and bulbs with perennials, groundcovers, and other plants to create eye-catching combinations.

Part of the pleasure of growing annuals and bulbs lies in their versatile natures. No matter where you live or what growing conditions you have to offer, you can find annuals and bulbs that will thrive where you plant them. Some prefer moist, shaded conditions, while others revel in sunny, dry spots. Cool-loving types add color to mild-winter or cool-spring gardens, while the heat-lovers thrive in the steamy conditions of summer and the warm temperatures of fall.

Of course, annuals and bulbs aren't just grown because they're practical and adaptable: They're beautiful, too! Their flowers come in a palette of colors to suit every gardener's fancy. Some also offer handsome foliage. Others are treasured for their fragrance, their nostalgic associations, or their charm as cut flowers. It's hard to imagine a garden that wouldn't benefit from the addition of a few more annuals and bulbs.

In this chapter, you'll learn all the basics you need to get started on successful flower gardening. "Understanding Annuals" on page 14 and "Understanding Bulbs" on page 16 explain the differences between these plants and how they grow in your garden. "Annuals and Bulbs in Your Garden" on page 18 is a gold mine of great ideas for growing these plants in all parts of your landscape—from formal flower beds and borders to casual cottage gardens and colorful container plantings.

While most annuals and bulbs willingly adapt to a range of conditions, choosing those that are best suited to the soil and light your garden has to offer is the real key to creating a great-looking garden. "Assessing Your Site" on page 22 explains how to evaluate your garden and determine the growing conditions you have available.

Once you understand your site, it's time to get down to the real business of gardening—deciding what you're going to grow and where it's going to go. You'll find lots of handy tips in the section on "Planning Your Plantings" on page 24. The last step before actually setting out the plants is deciding how to arrange them in pleasing groupings. For inspiration, try some of the tips in "Creating Great Combinations" on page 26. Then be prepared to enjoy your most beautiful garden ever!

Creating a great-looking flower garden starts with identifying the growing conditions your yard has to offer. Then you can select annuals and bulbs that will thrive there with little fussing from you.

Understanding Annuals

True annuals germinate, grow, flower, set seed, and die all in one season. Their single goal is to reproduce themselves. This is good news for the gardener, since it means that most annual plants will flower like mad to achieve this goal. Some of the best-known annuals—including petunias and marigolds—have achieved their popularity because of their free-flowering nature. If you use tricks such as deadheading (removing spent flowers) to prevent seed formation, many annuals will step up flower production and bloom well over an extended period until cold weather arrives.

The first hard frost usually kills the plants and

Marigolds are generally classified as half-hardy annuals. They prefer warm weather but can take a light frost in fall.

signals the end of the bloom season for that year. Although you'll need to replant most annuals the following spring to get another show, some will sprout from seed dropped by last year's plants. "Reseeding Annuals and Biennials" lists several species that can return for years after just one planting.

Besides these true annuals, there are a number of perennial plants that are often thought of as annuals. These include tropical perennials, such as zonal geraniums, or perennials that will flower the first season from seed, such as four-o'clocks (*Mirabilis jalapa*). These plants can live for years in frost-free climates, but, like true annuals, they meet their death at the hands of freezing temperatures in cold-winter climates. "Perennial Annuals" lists some of the perennial plants that are normally grown as annuals.

Kinds of Annuals

Annuals are sometimes further separated into three groups—hardy, half-hardy, and tender—based on their cold tolerance. It's useful to know which kind of annuals you're growing so you'll know how soon you can get away with planting the annuals in the spring. The catalog, seed packet, or plant tag should tell you whether your plant is hardy, half-hardy, or tender.

Hardy Annuals Hardy annuals include forget-me-nots (*Myosotis* spp.), pansies, snapdragons, and other plants that withstand several degrees of freezing temperatures. Most of these plants perform best during cool weather. They are often planted in early spring by gardeners in cold-winter areas or in winter by gardeners in the South and West. Some hardy annuals, such as ornamental kale, are also associated with cool fall weather.

Perennial Annuals

You may be surprised to discover that some of the most popular annuals are actually perennials! The plants listed below are grown as annuals in most climates, but they can live for years in mild or frost-free areas.

Begonia Semperflorens-cultorum hybrid (wax begonia)

Bellis perennis (English daisy)

Catharanthus roseus (Madagascar periwinkle)

Cheiranthus cheiri (wallflower)

Chrysanthemum frutescens (marguerite)

Coleus x *hybridus* (coleus)

Dianthus chinensis (China pink)

Eustoma grandiflorum (prairie gentian)

Gazania rigens (treasure flower)

Heliotropium arborescens (heliotrope)

Impatiens wallerana (impatiens)

Mirabilis jalapa (four-o'clock)

Pelargonium x *hortorum* (zonal geranium)

Rudbeckia hirta (gloriosa daisy)

Salvia farinacea (mealy-cup sage)

Salvia splendens (scarlet sage)

Senecio cineraria (dusty miller)

Torenia fournieri (wishbone flower)

Verbena x *hybrida* (garden verbena)

Viola x *wittrockiana* (pansy)

Shirley poppies (*Papaver rhoeas*) are hardy annuals. You can sow them in early spring, or even in fall in mild areas.

Half-hardy Annuals Half-hardy annuals fit somewhere in the middle of hardy and tender. They will often withstand a touch of frost near the beginning or end of the gardening season. Many of the most commonly grown annuals fit in this category.

A half-hardy designation is like yellow on a traffic signal: You need to use your judgment to decide when you can plant safely. If your spring has been a bit on the warm side and you're itching to plant—even though your average frost-free day has not yet arrived—you might just get away with planting half-hardy annuals. If you do, though, be prepared to cover them if cold night temperatures are predicted. Consider hedging your bets by planting out only part of your half-hardy seeds or transplants at one time; then wait a week or two to plant the rest.

Tender Annuals Tender annuals, originally from tropical or subtropical climates, can't stand a degree of frost. More than that, they often grow poorly during cold weather and may be stunted by prolonged exposure to temperatures below 50°F (10°C). For best results, wait until late spring to plant tender annuals, such as celosia (*Celosia* spp.) and Joseph's-coat (*Amaranthus tricolor*).

What Is a Biennial?

Biennials have much in common with annuals, but they differ in one major respect: They take 2 years to complete their life cycle. The first year after sowing, they produce a leaf structure, building energy for the next year. The second year they flower, set seed, and die. Common garden biennials include honesty (*Lunaria annua*), foxglove (*Digitalis purpurea*), and sweet William (*Dianthus barbatus*).

Reseeding Annuals and Biennials

Many gardeners count on self-sowing annuals and biennials for perennial pleasures. Far from being a nuisance, these reliable repeaters delight many gardeners with their perseverance and their ability to pop up in the most unexpected places. Exactly which plants will self-sow depends on your region, but the ones listed below are some of the most dependable reseeders.

Alcea rosea (hollyhock)
Amaranthus caudatus (love-lies-bleeding)
Calendula officinalis (pot marigold)
Centaurea cyanus (cornflower, bachelor's button)
Chrysanthemum parthenium (feverfew)
Cleome hasslerana (cleome)
Consolida ambigua (rocket larkspur)
Coreopsis tinctoria (calliopsis)
Cosmos bipinnatus (cosmos)
Digitalis purpurea (foxglove)
Eschscholzia californica (California poppy)
Helianthus annuus (common sunflower)
Iberis umbellata (annual candytuft)
Impatiens balsamina (garden balsam)
Ipomoea tricolor (morning glory)
Lobularia maritima (sweet alyssum)
Lunaria annua (honesty)
Mirabilis jalapa (four-o'clock)
Myosotis sylvatica (forget-me-not)
Nicotiana alata (flowering tobacco)
Nigella damascena (love-in-a-mist)
Papaver rhoeas (corn poppy)
Portulaca grandiflora (rose moss)
Sanvitalia procumbens (creeping zinnia)
Tithonia rotundifolia (Mexican sunflower)
Tropaeolum majus (nasturtium)
Verbascum bombyciferum (mullein)
Zinnia angustifolia (narrow-leaved zinnia)

Understanding Bulbs

There's a time and place in the garden for nearly every bulb. The dainty blooms of early bulbs such as crocus and snowdrops (*Galanthus* spp.) signal the beginning of the gardening season with their arrival. Daffodils, tulips, and other larger bulbs are the epitome of the spring garden, while gladioli, lilies, and others strut their stuff in the summer. Some, including fall crocus (*Colchicum autumnale*) and hardy cyclamen (*Cyclamen hederifolium*), flower very late, marking the transition to winter temperatures despite their fragile, spring-like appearance. If you choose carefully, you can have bulbs in bloom nearly year-round!

Bulbs flower at different times because they are naturally adapted to different growing conditions. Learning a little about how bulbs grow and the various kinds of bulbs will help you to understand more about growing these colorful and versatile plants in your garden.

Daffodils are traditional favorites for adding color to spring gardens. They bloom year after year with little care.

How Bulbs Grow

Over time, bulbs have developed in a unique way to cope with their environments. A bulbous plant stores energy and water below ground in an enlarged root or stem. This storage area allows the plant to grow and flower when the growing conditions are favorable and to ride out unfavorable weather in a dormant state.

Tulips, for example, evolved on the high plains of western Asia. Between the hot, dry summers and freezing winters, a tulip takes advantage of the two mildest seasons. It roots in fall, relying on late rains to pump moisture into the bulb. Aboveground growth begins in early spring, often before cold weather has completely retreated. Melting snow waters the emerging buds, and bright sunshine stimulates the leaves to store energy depleted by the flowering process. As hot, dry weather arrives, the bulb goes back into a dormant state.

Of course, bulbous plants come from environments all around the globe, so they don't all behave in the same manner. Some may be stimulated to grow by the return of the rainy season; others respond to the warmth of spring or summer. While you don't need to know exactly which conditions encourage a particular bulb to bloom, it's helpful to realize that all of your bulbs will go through some kind of seasonal cycle of growth and dormancy. The individual entries in the "Guide to Bulbs," starting on page 138, will explain the cycle for each bulb, so you'll know when to plant, when to expect flowers, and when to divide or move the bulb.

Kinds of Bulbs

Many different plants that have underground storage structures are grouped together under the general term "bulbs." But technically, these underground structures take on several forms, including true bulbs, corms, tubers, and rhizomes.

True Bulbs True bulbs, such as tulips, daffodils, lilies, and hyacinths, must reach a particular size before they can flower. A full-size bulb contains layers of food-storing scales surrounding a tiny flower, formed during the previous growing season. With sufficient water, nutrients, and light, the bulb will blossom reliably the first year; this

It's hard to match hybrid tulips for pure color power! To repeat the show every spring, you may need to replant with new bulbs each fall.

Both tulips and bluebells (*Hyacinthoides* spp.) grow from true bulbs.

The dainty pink flowers of hardy cyclamen (*Cyclamen* spp.) are produced by tubers, while crocus grow from corms.

makes true bulbs a good choice for beginning gardeners. Encouraging true bulbs—especially some tulips—to bloom in subsequent years is sometimes a little trickier. The specific growing requirements vary for different species, but most true bulbs are easy to grow and maintain for years.

bulb

True bulbs reproduce by two methods: by seed and by bulblets produced at the base of the mother bulb (or, in the case of some lilies, in the leaf axils of the stem).

Corms Corms, such as those of crocus or gladioli, resemble true bulbs on the outside. Cut one open, however, and you'll discover a big difference. A corm is solid—a reservoir of energy without an embryonic flower inside. Under favorable conditions, a corm draws on its stockpile of food to produce leaves and flowers from growth buds on the top of the corm. As it grows, a corm exhausts its resources and often, but not always, grows a new corm to replace the old one. Corms also reproduce by forming small new corms, called cormlets or cormels, around the main corm.

corm

Tubers Like corms, tubers are solid storage structures. But unlike corms, which form roots only at the bottom, tubers can sprout roots from "eyes" (buds) scattered over their surface. The one tuber everyone knows is the potato. Most other tubers bear

a resemblance to it, although some may be flatter or thinner. Caladiums and tuberous begonias grow from tubers. Dahlias grow from similar structures called tuberous roots.

Most tubers originated in areas where summer temperatures are fairly warm and rainfall is plentiful. They can adapt to a range of conditions as long as they have warmth and sufficient moisture. Many will not survive in frozen ground, so you'll need to dig them up in fall and store them indoors over winter. Most tubers can be cut or broken into pieces to increase your stock of a plant; just make sure each piece has one or more eyes so it can produce new shoots.

tuber

Rhizomes A rhizome is a fleshy, creeping stem that is sometimes visible at ground level but is often hidden underground. Roots are produced on the undersides of each rhizome. Perhaps the most recognizable rhizome belongs to the old-fashioned bearded iris; other examples include cannas and calla lilies (*Zantedeschia aethiopica*).

rhizome

Most rhizomes are planted horizontally, just below the soil surface, so the roots can easily grow down into the soil. You can increase rhizomes easily by cutting them into pieces and replanting them.

Annuals and Bulbs in Your Garden

You could spend a lifetime exploring the rich diversity of annuals and bulbs. With their range of colors, heights, habits, and bloom times, there are annuals and bulbs for every purpose and every garden. If you're looking for exciting ways to enjoy these plants in your yard, here are some ideas to get you started.

Annual Additions

Many beginning gardeners draw their inspiration from public parks and gardens. Few American parks go without the summertime institution of brilliantly colored annuals laid out in formal blocks, rows, or patterns. These eye-catching displays tempt the neophyte to experiment with a few plants at home, almost inevitably lining up their annuals in rows.

Unfortunately, mimicking large public plantings is rarely satisfactory in a home garden, since the scale and budget are inevitably reduced. When you have to pay for the plants, prepare the soil, and maintain the garden, large plantings usually aren't realistic. And the formal row arrangements that look fine in a public garden may look awkward and overly formal in a backyard setting.

Rows can be satisfactory for some purposes: along sidewalks leading to front entries, as a crisp edging to delineate paths and beds, or for formal displays to match a particular architectural theme. But many of us line things up simply because we don't trust our design skills. A straight line seems like a safe bet, so we don't go any further. But if you're willing to

Besides making a great garden accent, globe amaranth (*Gomphrena globosa*) dries well for flower arrangements.

be a little more creative, you'll be amazed at all the fun ways you can add annuals to your landscape.

Annuals Alone In some places, you may choose to go with a basic all-annuals bed. Plants that have been bred or selected exclusively for a certain height or color are ideal for this kind of design. These compact, uniform annuals, such as dwarf marigolds, zinnias, or scarlet sage (*Salvia splendens*), lend themselves to lines as well as to mass plantings of geometric shapes.

A single color of one annual—massed together—can make an eye-catching landscape accent. This kind of planting is useful for long-distance viewing (such as from the street), for marking drives or entry gates, or for drawing attention to a door or entryway.

But keep in mind that color doesn't have to be shocking to get attention. The standard American

Planted in groups, compact zinnias provide a colorful, season-long show in flower beds and borders.

Combining different colors of the same annual adds variety and excitement to a mass planting.

attention-getter—sheets of red geraniums or scarlet sage—definitely has room for improvement. Expanses of startling color may be exciting for a few weeks, but they aren't particularly easy on the nerves when you have to look at them month after month. By varying the main color (such as different shades of red and pink) or by adding accents of complementary or contrasting tones (like pale yellow marigolds with deep purple petunias), the picture becomes more pleasurable throughout the season. "Annuals for Color Theme Gardens" on page 36 has lots of great ideas you can use to plan your bed and border plantings around your favorite flower colors.

Annuals and bulbs are ideal for filling new garden areas until you have the time and money for permanent plantings.

Annuals as Accents Fast-growing and relatively inexpensive annuals are invaluable for providing quick color to new gardens. But don't forget that they can enhance an existing landscape as well. Repeated plantings of a particular type or color can provide a note of continuity to an established framework of shrubs and trees.

Experimenting with new colors and combinations allows a new twist on the theme each year, without the expense of changing the framework itself. Annual additions also enliven established borders of perennials. Purists may object to including annuals in herbaceous plantings, but there's no law against it. While compact bedding types may look awkward next to larger perennials, many annuals have an airy grace that earns them a place among the most beautiful border plants. Foxgloves (*Digitalis purpurea*), hollyhocks (*Alcea rosea*), and gloriosa daisies (*Rudbeckia hirta*) are a few of the many annuals and biennials that make fine partners for perennials. As a bonus, long-blooming annuals can provide a steady supply of color to fill in as their perennial companions come into and go out of flower.

When deciding what to grow with your annuals, though, don't just stop with perennials. In an "everything goes" cottage garden, you can combine annuals with all kinds of other plants—bulbs, shrubs, grasses, herbs, trees, and whatever else looks good to you. There are no rules here; simply put each plant where it will thrive and complement its neighbors.

Annual flowers are also a fun addition to a traditional vegetable garden, adding a bit of color or filling in after early-season crops are harvested. Some annuals, such as scarlet runner beans (*Phaseolus coccineus*), nasturtiums, and sunflowers, even have good flavor to match their good looks. For more fun ideas on incorporating annuals into your garden, see "Annuals for Beds and Borders" on page 30.

Annuals in Containers One of the most popular ways to bring excitement to any garden is with containers. These plantings may vary from year to year and even season to season. Pansies can dominate in cool weather, for instance, while ageratums or geraniums take over during the heat of summer.

A large pot, overflowing with a carefully selected variety of flowering and foliage plants, is a classic way to show off annuals. Even with small containers, you can make hundreds of different combinations to liven up decks, patios, balconies, and other living areas. You can have multiple pots that repeat the same theme throughout your garden, or change the plantings to set a new mood. Instead of combining several different plants in one container, you could group several smaller pots of individual plants. This is a good way to group favorite colors, pick up predominate colors from surrounding beds, or try out new color combinations. For more ideas, see "Annuals for Container Gardens" on page 32.

Annuals for Scented Gardens For many gardeners, fragrance is an important consideration when deciding which annuals to grow and where to put them. Sweet alyssum (*Lobularia maritima*) smells of honey on a hot afternoon, while night-scented stock (*Matthiola longipetala* subsp. *bicornis*) wafts a sweet scent on an evening breeze. Scented blooms are delightful in containers or beds near windows or outdoor sitting areas. If you usually spend your summer evenings outdoors, you might want to concentrate on evening-scented blooms; if you're only outdoors during the day, flowers that are fragrant during the evening may not be useful to you. "Annuals for Fragrance" on page 40 offers more tips on choosing and enjoying scented flowers and foliage in your garden.

Annuals for Cut Flowers If you enjoy bringing your garden flowers indoors, consider starting a separate cutting garden. That way, you can have a generous supply of flowers for cutting without raiding your more visible displays. Annuals that are good for cutting produce lots of flowers and last well

If you enjoy fragrant flowers, tuck sweet peas and other scented annuals into your beds and borders.

indoors; these include zinnias, snapdragons, cosmos, pot marigolds (*Calendula officinalis*), China aster (*Callistephus chinensis*), and rocket larkspur (*Consolida ambigua*). Scented flowers are also delightful in arrangements. So-called everlasting flowers—such as globe amaranth (*Gomphrena globosa*), statice (*Limonium sinuatum*), and strawflowers (*Helichrysum bracteatum*)—are an important part of many cutting gardens, since their beauty lives on into the winter in dried arrangements. For more information on growing and harvesting annuals for arrangements, see "Annuals for Cutting Gardens" on page 38.

Annuals for Garden Challenges Annuals are adaptable and easy to grow, making them the ideal for all kinds of gardening challenges. If you have just moved into a house, you could fill the garden with annuals for a year or two while you decide on your long-term plans for the landscape. (For more details, see "Annuals as Fillers" on page 34.) Or, if you rent a home with a plot of ground, annuals allow you to enjoy flower gardening without the more permanent investment in perennials. Annuals are great for city gardens, since they can make the most of compact spaces and less-than-ideal growing sites. Tall annuals and annual vines are also excellent as temporary screens to hide unsightly views, objectionable fences, stumps, or neighbors; see "Annuals for Screens" on page 35 for ideas on using these plants effectively.

Bulb Magic

Like annuals, bulbs are often used in masses in large-scale landscapes. While it's difficult to re-create those grand displays with limited space and money, well-

Moisture-loving monkey flower (*Mimulus* x *hybridus*) is a dramatic addition to soggy spots in the garden.

Add sparkle to beds and borders by pairing spring bulbs with early annuals.

Tulips, grape hyacinths (*Muscari* spp.), and many other bulbs are excellent in arrangements; grow some extras for cutting.

chosen bulbs can create equally stunning effects in many parts of the home garden.

Bulbs in Beds and Borders It's hard to beat bulbs for early color. What could be more welcome to a winter-weary gardener than a patch of brightly colored crocus by the back door? While bulb flowers are pretty on their own, you can also combine them with other early-blooming perennials or shrubs to create stunning effects, such as a golden flood of daffodils beneath a blooming forsythia. Many spring-blooming bulbs enliven planted areas beneath trees, performing their fabulous show before the trees have leafed out. The bulbs finish just as the shade-loving ferns, hostas, or annuals come on stage.

Bulbs are especially useful when tucked into perennial plantings, since they get the bloom season off to an early start. Summer beds make a great place for showcasing tender bulbs, such as cannas and gladioli, among annuals or perennials. Later-blooming bulbs such as lilies and dahlias add height and color to mid- and late-season borders. For more ideas on how to use bulbs in flower gardens, see "Planting Bulbs in Beds and Borders" on page 128.

Bulbs for Fragrance and Flower Arrangements Hyacinths, Madonna lilies (*Lilium candidum*), tuberoses (*Polianthes tuberosa*), and some other bulbs offer sweet fragrances that are delightful both outdoors and indoors. Just use moderation when cutting these flowers for arrangements; a single bloom can pleasantly scent a room, but a mass of them can be overpowering.

Even without fragrance, many hardy and tender bulbs are excellent for cutting gardens. You could start the season with tulips and daffodils, followed by summer snowflake (*Leucojum aestivum*) and lilies, as well as gladioli and dahlias. In the South, you can even grow amaryllis (*Hippeastrum* hybrids) outdoors for cut flowers. "Bulbs for Cutting Gardens" on page 122 offers more details for growing and handling bulbs for cutting.

Bulbs in Containers Bulbs are perfect for pots, alone for a touch of movable spring color or combined with annuals for a longer season of interest. They can also be potted up in fall for later indoor pleasure. Tender bulbs, such as amaryllis and paperwhite narcissus, are very easy to grow and flower on the windowsill with little fussing. Hardy bulbs, such as tulips and hyacinths, need to be potted and chilled for several months to give them a condensed form of winter before bringing them inside. This process is known as "forcing," although the bulbs aren't forced to do anything except bloom a bit ahead of schedule, either in the house or on the patio. Depending on where you live, there are different methods of forcing bulbs; you'll find all the details in "Bulbs for Indoor Bloom" on page 114.

Assessing Your Site

To have a beautiful, healthy garden, you don't have to be born with a "green thumb." The real secret to creating a great-looking garden is a keen sense of observation. You need to know what kind of growing conditions your yard has available—how much light, what kind of climate, and what kind of soil—so you can choose annuals and bulbs that will grow and thrive there with little extra help from you.

Sun and Shade

If you've lived in the same house for years, you probably know which parts of your yard are sunny and which are shady. If you've just started gardening or if you've recently moved to a new home, however, figuring this out is your first step to planning a good garden.

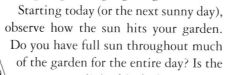

Starting today (or the next sunny day), observe how the sun hits your garden. Do you have full sun throughout much of the garden for the entire day? Is the light blocked on one or more sides by buildings, other structures, or evergreen trees? Through the seasons, do deciduous trees block more sunlight, or does the changing angle of the sun open areas up to more sun?

To get the most accurate picture of the sun and shade patterns, you really need to observe your yard over a full year. Make a rough map of your property and duplicate it so you have several copies. Throughout the year—maybe once a season or once a month—take a fresh copy of your map, record the date, and mark which spots are sunny or shady. Also note which spots are shaded for part of the day and sunbaked for the rest. After a year, you'll

Planning your gardens on paper can help you create a landscape that's practical as well as beautiful.

If you have a hot, sunny site with dry or sandy soil, look for drought-tolerant annuals, such as creeping zinnia.

have good records to help you plan future plantings.

Of course, this doesn't mean you're not allowed to plant anything until you've watched the garden for a whole year. Many annuals are surprisingly tolerant of a range of conditions, and they may grow fine even if the site turns out to be a little sunnier or shadier than you expected. But once you have your notes, you can fine-tune future plant choices to give your annuals and bulbs the conditions they like best. To find out the sun or shade preferences for specific plants, check the individual entries in the "Guide to Annuals," starting on page 58, or the "Guide to Bulbs," starting on page 138.

Climate Considerations

Knowing your climate is another important planning tool. When you're growing annuals, you should know the dates of the average first and last frosts in your area. These dates will help you decide when it's safe to sow or transplant. They'll also tell you the length of growing season you can expect. Some flowers need a long season to reach flowering stage and are not always viable options for short-season or high-altitude gardeners. You can usually get this information from gardeners in your neighborhood or from your local Cooperative Extension Service office.

If you're growing bulbs outdoors, you need to know what hardiness zone you live in. The entire country is assigned to hardiness zones, based on average annual low temperatures. You can find out what zone you live in by checking the USDA Plant Hardiness Zone Map on page 154. Catalog descriptions and the individual plant entries in the "Guide to Bulbs," starting on page 138, will tell you which zones a particular bulb is adapted to. While these recommendations aren't foolproof, they will help you determine which bulbs should survive the winter in your area.

For either annuals or bulbs, temperatures and frost dates aren't the only aspect of climate that's important; you also need to consider rainfall. Unless your area receives regular rainfall through the growing season, you'll have to either provide water for your plants or select plants that have low water requirements. Of course, even areas that usually get rain will have dry spells now and then. Consider installing an irrigation system of some sort (maybe just a soaker hose that you can leave in place during the season), or be prepared to hand water daily during periods of high heat and low rainfall.

In mild-winter areas, gladiolus corms can stay in the ground all year; in cold climates, you'll have to dig them in fall for winter storage indoors.

Soil and Site Conditions

When you're growing annuals and bulbs in pots, it's fairly easy to adjust the soil mix to meet the needs of particular plants. But when you're gardening in the ground, you'll have better results for less work if you choose plants that will thrive in your existing soil conditions.

You can learn a lot about your garden by feeling the soil. Take a handful of moist (not muddy) soil, squeeze it, and open your hand. Then follow these guidelines to determine your soil type.

• If the soil crumbles, it's on the sandy side. Sandy soils drain well but don't hold much water or many nutrients. Drought-tolerant annuals,. including California poppy (*Eschscholzia californica*), rose moss (*Portulaca grandiflora*), and creeping zinnia (*Sanvitalia procumbens*), are ideal for sandy sites. Many bulbs also thrive in light, sandy soils.

• If the soil forms a clump but breaks apart when you tap it lightly, it's on the loamy side. Loamy soils tend to hold a good balance of water and nutrients, so they

When squeezed in your hand, sandy soil tends to stay loose, while clay soil usually forms a ball.

can support a variety of annuals and bulbs.

If the soil stays in a clump even when you tap it, it's probably high in clay. Clays tend to be waterlogged when wet and very hard when dry. While some annuals and bulbs can adapt to heavy, clay soils, it's usually best to dig in lots of organic matter to provide more hospitable growing conditions.

You'll find more information on handling any of these kinds of soil in "Preparing the Soil and Planting" on page 49 and "Planting Bulbs" on page 128.

Make the Most of Microclimates

Each garden might have several unique growing areas, normally called microclimates. Shady nooks fit into this category. So do hot spots, like beds that get extra heat from walls or paving.

As you plan your plantings, look for these special spots where particular plants may thrive. A sunny, south-facing bed along a brick terrace, for instance, could hold extra warmth for a great show of crocus and pansies in early spring. The same site, though, would probably be too hot for the pansies in summer, so you'd need to replace them with heat-tolerant annuals, such as treasure flower (*Gazania rigens*) or rose moss (*Portulaca grandiflora*). Observing your garden through the seasons and identifying these microclimates will help you choose the most appropriate plants for each site and season.

Planning Your Plantings

With so many enticing seed and nursery catalogs around, it's tempting to just grab a pen and a checkbook and start ordering everything that catches your eye. While most gardeners have experienced this weakness at least once (or—to be more honest—on a regular basis!), buying without some kind of plan is usually a formula for disappointment. The plants that looked so perfect in the photos may not be right for your site or climate or for the bloom times that you hoped for. To have a successful garden, you need to do a little planning before you make your purchases.

There are two ways to approach your planning. One way is to have an idea of what you want to grow and choose a site on your property that's suitable. Another way to plan is to decide where you want to have a garden and then pick the plants that are adapted to those growing conditions. This approach may seem more limiting, but it's a good way to make sure your plants will grow well in the site you've chosen for them. Both techniques have their merits, and most gardeners end up using both at different times. Either way, the key is always to match the plants to the place they're growing.

When you combine plants that have similar needs, it's easy to provide the right care to keep them in top condition.

Deciding Where to Plant

If you have your heart set on growing particular plants, your site choices are probably limited. You need a spot that can provide the right amount of light and the right soil conditions for your plants.

If you don't have particular plants in mind, you have a lot more freedom in site selection. Here are some points to consider when deciding on a planting area.

- **How much sun does it get?** Many annuals and bulbs thrive in full sun, but some adapt to or even need at least partial shade.
- **What is the soil like?** Is it loose and sandy, hard and clayey, very wet, very dry, or very rocky? There's an annual or bulb for just about every site, but fairly loose, well-drained soil that isn't too dry or rocky is ideal. If you're stuck with miserable, compacted clay soil, you could excavate the area and refill it with good topsoil. For very clayey, rocky, or wet sites, raised beds are another alternative.
- **Is it easy to reach?** A flower bed at the end of your driveway or out by your mailbox may seem like a nice idea, but it could be a hassle to maintain—especially if you have to lug water out to it regularly. Try to keep plantings closer to the house, where you can reach them for easy watering, grooming, and general maintenance.

Deciduous trees make ideal companions for early bulbs. The bulbs get full sun in spring and go dormant by the time the expanding tree leaves block the light.

If tulips are on your must-have list, look for a planting site that has well-drained soil and plenty of sun.

Growing bulbs and annuals in containers lets you move the plants around to experiment with combinations.

- **What's growing there now?** Neglected areas will have to be cleared of weeds. If the area is currently in lawn, you'll need to remove the turf or hire someone else to do it. Clearing out overgrown shrub plantings can be an even bigger task. However, just about any site can be prepared for planting if you're willing to put the time and effort into it.

Deciding What to Plant

Chances are good that you already have some idea of what you want to grow in your garden. As you flip through books, magazines, and catalogs for more ideas, it's fun to make a wish list of plants you'd like to try. Along with the names, you'll also want to note the characteristics of each plant, including its light and soil preferences, height, color, and bloom time.

If you have already chosen a site for your garden, the next step is to go through your list and select the plants that are adapted to the site conditions. "Creating Great Combinations" on page 26 offers some tips on grouping your selections based on heights, colors, and bloom times. If you'd rather grow your annuals and bulbs for a particular purpose— for cutting, perhaps, or fragrance—you'll have to consider the needs of each plant you want to grow and then find a spot in your yard where it will thrive. In "Annuals and Bulbs in Your Garden," starting on page 18, you'll find suggestions of excellent annuals and bulbs for particular purposes.

Putting It on Paper

Once you've chosen a site and know what you want to plant, you may wish to lay out your plan on paper. It's not always necessary—in fact, some gardeners prefer to follow their creative urges with plants in hand, designing on the spot. But planning on paper does have one distinct advantage, at least for new gardeners: It

can help you figure out how many plants to buy.

The number of plants you need to fill a given space depends on the size of the bed and the spread of the plant. Follow these steps:

1. Determine the area of the planting bed. Measure the length and the width of the bed in inches, then multiply the two numbers to get the area in square inches. If, for example, your bed is 24 x 36 inches, you'd multiply 24 and 36 to get 864 square inches.

2. Next, figure out how far apart the plants should be. You can find the spread of individual plants in the "Guide to Annuals," starting on page 58 and the "Guide to Bulbs," starting on page 138. If you're growing several different kinds of annuals in one bed, you'll need to use some average spacing for your calculations. In this example, let's say you're planting only one kind of hybrid marigold, and it needs to be spaced 6 inches apart.

3. Now, multiply the required spacing of the plant (in inches) by the same number to find the number of square inches for each plant. (This will allow room for the plant to spread and just touch its neighbors.) Your marigold, for instance, would need 36 square inches (6 x 6 inches).

4. Last, divide the total area of the bed (864 square inches, in this example) by the number of square inches required by each plant (36 square inches for each marigold). The answer (24, in this case) is the number of plants you need to buy.

As you gain gardening experience, you probably will be able to guess how many plants you need without going through this formula. You may choose to plant a little closer together for a more full look or a little farther apart if your plants tend to get too crowded.

Creating Great Combinations

There are no hard-and-fast rules in gardening. Certainly there are guidelines when it comes to good plant culture. But when it comes to garden aesthetics, it's ludicrous to lay down the law.

After all, our tastes in flowers are as individual as our taste in clothing. Who would argue against the right of a gardener to wear a Hawaiian print shirt with plaid Bermuda shorts or to grow bright red snapdragons with pale blue ageratums? It might not work for most of us, but we all march to a different beat. Understanding a few basic design principles, however, is helpful for planting a pleasing garden.

Choose Compatible Plants

The first step to any good combination is choosing plants that prefer the same conditions. You might think that bachelor's buttons (*Centaurea cyanus*) would look charming with impatiens, for instance, but they probably won't grow well together; one needs full sun and the other prefers shade. Know the site conditions you have available, and stick with plants you know can thrive there.

Think about Bloom Time

Bloom season is another important consideration. Annuals make great companions for bulbs, since the annuals can fill in the garden space left when the bulbs go dormant. But if you want the plants to be in flower at the same time, look for those that have similar bloom seasons.

Pick Plants with Different Heights

Unless you're planting a bed with just one kind of annual or bulb, its usually most pleasing to include

Bluebells (*Hyacinthoides* spp.) and other early bulbs blend beautifully with spring-flowering shrubs.

plants of different sizes. Taller plants generally look best in the back of a bed or in the center of a bed that is viewed from several vantage points (such as an island bed in the middle of a lawn). Most seed packets or nursery tags will give you an idea of how tall a plant should grow. The actual height in your garden may differ somewhat, based on the available growing conditions, but at least you'll have a rough idea.

Include a Variety of Shapes

Combining plants with different shapes is another way to add interest to your garden. Some plants and flowers are spiky and rigid (think of hyacinths or snapdragons); some, such as love-in-a-mist (*Nigella damascena*) and flowering tobacco (*Nicotiana alata*), are more graceful and loose in habit. Impatiens, marigolds, and many other plants have a compact, rounded shape. It's hard to go wrong if you include some plants of each shape in your garden.

Low-growing pansies make a charming carpet under tulips, and the color combinations are almost unlimited.

Grouping spiky, bushy, and trailing plants gives container gardens a rich, full look and lots of interest.

The spiky flower form of biennial foxgloves (*Digitalis* spp.) complements rounded flowers, such as roses.

Consider the Colors

Colors can be harmonious or contrasting. Some gardeners prefer pastels, while others like primary hues—rich reds, sunny yellows, and bright blues.

If you're planning your garden around your favorite color, you'll probably want to use many variations of that color—maybe pale and medium pinks with reds, or cream and yellow flowers with deep golds. In a mixed-color planting, though, it's generally best to avoid combining pastels and strong colors.

Until you gain confidence in creating pleasing color combinations, you may wish to plan separate beds or pots for pastels and bold colors. You'll avoid the "explosion in a paint factory" syndrome and learn which combinations please you most. Go with the hues that you naturally prefer, but leave your options open to try something new and daring. Everybody enjoys a Hawaiian shirt once in a while!

If soft pastels are too tame for your taste, you can create eye-catching effects by pairing bright colors.

A Combination Case Study

Once you start grouping plants with an eye for compatible heights, habits, and colors, you'll develop a feeling for which ones could look good together. But when you're a beginner, the idea of planning pleasing combinations may be a little intimidating.

To see how easy it can be, let's look at one simple combination and figure out why it works. We'll start with a patch of Madagascar periwinkle (*Catharanthus roseus*), with its flat, five-petaled, deep pink blossoms. Behind that, we'll add a group of mealy-cup sage (*Salvia farinacea*) for its spikes of small, blue flowers. And to enhance this duo, let's tuck in a few plants of airy yellow cosmos (*Cosmos sulphureus*) toward the back.

Why does this trio work? First, all three annuals share the need for a sunny spot and perform best in the summer heat. The shape, texture, and height of each plant is different but compatible; the flower sizes and shapes also vary. Finally, the colors—pink, blue, and yellow—work well together; each contrasts with the other, but none is so strong that it overwhelms the others.

If you really like this combination, you could create a whole bed of just these three kinds of plants. Or you could expand it by adding other compatible plants—perhaps the blue-flowered, low-growing annual lobelia or a dramatic yellow Asiatic hybrid lily to serve as a focal point. Once you start trying out new flower and foliage combinations, the fun never ends!

ANNUALS IN YOUR GARDEN

You just can't beat annuals for adding easy-care color to all parts of your yard. They offer a wealth of dazzling flowers and fabulous foliage without the commitment of more permanent plantings, like perennials and shrubs. With annuals, you can indulge your creative urges by trying new arrangements and color combinations each year or easily re-create favorite plantings from previous years.

The greatest feature of annuals can be summed up in one word: versatility. Take a well-known, easy-to-grow annual like the marigold. Individual plants can add spots of cheerful color to a window box, patio planter, or hanging basket. A mass of marigolds in its own bed creates an eye-catching landscape feature. A row of marigolds creates a tidy edging for a walkway or provides a steady supply of fresh flowers for a cutting garden. A small group can sparkle near a doorway, brighten a foundation planting of dark evergreens, or highlight an important garden feature, such as a birdbath or statue. Marigolds can even accent established perennial plantings with season-long color, fill in around new perennials while they're getting established, or cover the bare soil left by fading spring bulbs.

It's downright amazing to realize that just one common annual can give you all of these options. And it's even more exciting when you consider that there are hundreds of annuals for you to choose from. But the benefits of adding annuals to your garden don't stop there. Besides their versatility, annuals also offer you a valuable chance to gain confidence in planning color combinations. You can experiment with all kinds of

wild or soothing color combinations without the commitment required for a more permanent perennial border. And if you make a jarring mistake with annuals, you can replace them, transplant them, or even tear them out and compost them without feeling guilty about the cost. When you discover combinations that you're really happy with, you can easily repeat them for great results each year.

In this chapter, you'll find specific suggestions for gardening with annuals in all parts of your landscape. "Annuals for Beds and Borders" on page 30 offers tips on growing annuals alone or mixed with perennials, bulbs, and other plants. "Annuals for Container Gardens" on page 32 tells how to plan and plant exciting and attractive container gardens. If you're looking for annuals to fill in your garden while new groundcovers, shrubs, or perennials get established, check out "Annuals as Fillers" on page 34. And for suggestions of fast-growing, tall annuals and annual vines to provide privacy and quick color, see "Annuals for Screens" on page 35.

If colorful flowers and fabulous fragrance are what you're after, there's lots of advice on these annuals, too. "Annuals for Color Theme Gardens" on page 36 has tips on creating color-based plantings, like a white garden or a "hot" border of bright reds, yellows, and oranges. "Annuals for Cutting Gardens" on page 38 offers ideas for annuals that make excellent cut flowers. For hints on selecting sweet-smelling flowers and foliage, see "Annuals for Fragrance" on page 40. And if herbs are your fancy, you'll want to read "Annuals for Herb Gardens" on page 41.

Flowering tobacco (*Nicotiana alata*) and other easy annuals can blend well in just about any garden setting. Plant them alone in masses or mix them with other plants in beds, borders, and container plantings.

Annuals for Container Gardens

Annuals make perfect container plants. They grow quickly, flower profusely, and provide a long season of good looks. Some also offer distinctive foliage, while others perfume the air with their sweet scents. Groups of small- and medium-sized containers create charming spots of movable color; large planters can showcase a stunning mix of colorful annuals in a relatively small space. Window boxes and hanging baskets are other options for displaying a wide range of flowering and foliage annuals.

Picking Annuals for Containers

As with any kind of garden, the first step to planning successful container plantings is choosing plants that have similar growth needs. If you have a shady area, impatiens, monkey flower (*Mimulus* x *hybridus*), and other shade-lovers are your best bets. Sunny spots can

support a wider range of colorful annuals, including treasure flower (*Gazania rigens*), mealy-cup sage (*Salvia farinacea*), and narrow-leaved zinnia (*Zinnia angustifolia*).

When planning a container garden—whether it is a pot, hanging basket, window box, or planter—you also need to consider the ultimate height of the annuals you select. As a general guideline, try to choose annuals that are the same height or smaller than the height of the container; otherwise, the planting may look top-heavy.

Single-annual containers can be pleasing, but mixed plantings of three or four different annuals are even more exciting. While the exact plants you pick to grow together is up to you, there are some basic guidelines you can follow to create a successful container planting. First, select a "star" plant. Base your container planting around one centerpiece plant—perhaps a bushy marguerite daisy (*Chrysanthemum frutescens*), a free-flowering tuberous begonia, or a bold ornamental cabbage. Then choose a "supporting cast" to complement the star plant and fill out the container. Try one or two with bold leaves or an upright habit—such as coleus or dusty miller—and one or two that sprawl or trail—such as edging lobelia (*Lobelia erinus*) or creeping zinnia (*Sanvitalia procumbens*).

Caring for Container Annuals

Container plants share closer quarters than garden plants, so they need some special care to stay lush and lovely. The first step to successful container growing is choosing a good container. Large pots tend to provide the best conditions for growth, since they hold

---

Wonderful Window Boxes

Nothing adds country charm to a house like lush window boxes dripping with cascades of colorful flowers and foliage. While the same general principles of container planting apply here, there are a few special tips to keep in mind to plan and maintain great-looking window boxes.

- **Consider the site.** Before you put up any window boxes, make sure you'll be able to reach them easily for watering and maintenance. Because window boxes are so visible, it's especially important to keep them well groomed; that means regularly removing spent flowers.

- **Stick with short plants.** Window boxes are usually planted to be seen from the outside, but you also need to consider the view from the inside. It's generally best to stick with plants no taller than about 8 inches (20 cm); those much taller than that can block your view.

- **Choose compatible colors.** Look for flower and foliage colors that complement those of the house and trim. Silvers and whites look crisp and cool against warm-toned brick, for instance, while blues and purples look pretty against cream colors, and pinks and yellows add life to somber gray siding.

Ornamental cabbage (*Brassica oleracea*) looks great in containers and can last well past the first fall frost.

When pansies or other spring annuals start to fade, replace them with summer annuals to keep planters looking good all season.

A large container can support a pleasing mixture of bushy and trailing plants.

more soil, nutrients, and water, but they are also quite heavy if you need to move or hang them. Pots or baskets that are about 8 inches (20 cm) deep can usually hold enough soil for good growth without getting too heavy. If you don't plan to move the planter, it can be as big as you want; containers as large as half-barrels will give you ample planting space for a wide variety of annuals.

Fill your container with a general potting mix that you buy at your local nursery or garden center. Straight garden soil is generally not suitable for containers, since it will pack down with repeated watering. Commercial potting mixes are easy to use, and they can support a variety of different plants.

Set your plants into the container soil, firm them in, and water to keep the soil moist through the season. Container gardens dry out quickly, so you may need to water every day during hot weather. Very small pots, small- and medium-sized clay containers, and hanging baskets dry out especially quickly; you may have to water these as often as twice a day.

If a pot or basket dries out completely, you still may be able to save the plants. Set the pot or basket in a larger container filled with water, let it sit there for an hour or two, and then set the pot or basket in a shady spot for a few hours until the plants perk up again. Then move the pot or basket back to its original spot, but be extra careful to keep those container plants well watered from then on.

Besides regular watering, the other key to lush-

looking containers is regular fertilizing. Give them a boost by watering them with diluted fish emulsion or compost tea (made by soaking a shovelful of finished compost in a bucket of water for about a week, then straining out the soaked compost). Start in late spring by feeding once every 2 weeks, then judge the containers in midsummer. If plants look lush but aren't flowering well, change to fertilizing once every 3 weeks. If the plants look somewhat spindly, start fertilizing every week. If the plants seem to be growing and flowering well, stick with the 2-week schedule.

If pots or baskets dry out, soak them in a bucket of water.

Misting or watering with liquid fertilizer will keep plants vigorous.

Keep your container plantings in peak condition by regularly removing spent flowers and old or yellowed leaves.

Try a colorful planting of low-growing annuals as a ground-cover around new tree and shrub plantings.

New gardens may look rather bare the first year or two. Annuals can cover the soil until perennials get established.

Annuals as Fillers

When you start any new garden, one of the hardest parts of the process is waiting for plants to fill in. This is especially true with perennial and shrub beds, since these plants can take 3 or 4 years to really get established and look like anything. New groundcover plantings can appear pretty sparse for the first few years, too. While you need to allow ample space for these plants to fill in as they mature, the bare soil in between is boring and empty, and it provides an open invitation for weeds to get started.

While mulch can suppress weeds, it doesn't add much excitement to a new planting. That's where filler annuals come in handy. A few seed packets of quick-growing annuals can provide welcome color and excitement for minimal cost. Sweet alyssum (*Lobularia maritima*), flowering tobacco (*Nicotiana alata*), and cornflower (*Centaurea cyanus*) are a few great fille annuals that can quickly cover the soil and deprive weed seeds of the light they need to grow. Many annuals may also self-sow to provide cover in succeeding years, gradually yielding space to expanding perennials.

Fillers for Flower Beds

If you're looking for annuals to fill in around new perennial plantings, choose those with a similar range of heights and colors as the perennials will have. Select a few short or trailing annuals for the front of the border, a few medium-sized plants for the middle of the border, and a few tall annuals for the back. While you could sow annual seed directly into the ground around the perennials, it's often easier to start with annual transplants.

Some good filler annuals, such as cleome (*Cleome hasslerana*) and cornflower, will drop seed and come back year after year. If your annuals do reseed, thin the seedlings to allow the expanding perennials room to develop.

Fillers for Groundcovers

Low-growing annuals such as sweet alyssum, rose moss (*Portulaca grandiflora*), and baby-blue-eyes (*Nemophila menziesii*) can be excellent fillers for young groundcover plantings. Stick with one kind of annual for a uniform effect. In this case, its just as easy to scatter seed around the groundcover plants, although you could also set out annual transplants in the available spaces instead. While many low-growing annuals will self-sow, you may want to scatter some fresh annual seed over the planting for the first few springs until the groundcover fills in.

Fillers for Foundation Plantings

New foundation plantings also benefit from annuals the first few years as they develop. Shrubs and groundcovers may take over their allotted space in a few years, but a carpet of annuals is most welcome in the meantime. A few market packs of your favorite annuals will be easy to plant, and the resulting flowers and foliage will provide infinitely more interest than a dull covering of bark chips.

Annuals for Screens

While the word "annual" commonly brings to mind compact, small plants like petunias and marigolds, there are a number of fast-growing annuals that can reach amazing heights of 6 feet (180 cm) or more in a single season. There are also annual vines, the twining stems of which quickly cover trellises for welcome shade and privacy. With these great plants to choose from, why spend another season staring at your neighbors' yards—or your neighbors, for that matter? Screen them off with fast-growing annuals.

Tall Annuals

Grow tall annuals in your yard to block or cover unattractive features, such as dog runs, alleys, or clothesline poles. Or plant a row or mass of tall annuals to create a "neighbor-friendly" temporary fence that delineates your property line or separates different areas of your garden. Some top-notch tall annuals include castor bean (*Ricinus communis*), summer cypress (*Kochia scoparia*), hollyhocks (*Alcea rosea*), sunflowers (*Helianthus annuus*), and Mexican sunflower (*Tithonia rotundifolia*). For more information on growing these high-risers, see their individual entries in the "Guide to Annuals," starting on page 58.

Annual Vines

A leafy curtain of annual vines is an ideal way to ensure privacy on a porch or patio without appearing to be unneighborly. Flowering vines also add a quaint, old-fashioned touch to the most ordinary support. A cloak of morning glories can convert a ho-hum garden shed into a charming garden feature, while a mass of scarlet runner bean will accent an arch or liven up a lamppost.

Most annual vines cover territory in a hurry. You can

Black-eyed Susan vine climbs quickly to cover fences or trellises with bright blooms from summer into fall.

easily train them to climb a wooden or wire trellis, chain-link fences, lattice work, or even strong twine. Tall wooden or bamboo stakes also make effective supports. While annual vines are usually lighter than woody vines (such as wisteria or trumpet creeper), they can put on a lot of growth in one season, so supply a sturdy support. Unlike clinging vines such as ivy, annual vines mostly climb with tendrils or twining stems, so don't expect them to scamper up a bare wall without assistance.

Morning glories (*Ipomoea tricolor*) have long been loved for their heart-shaped leaves and beautiful, trumpet-shaped flowers. The closely related moonflower (*Ipomoea alba*) is another popular vine; it offers large, white, heavily fragrant flowers that open in the evening. Besides being covered with clusters of colorful blooms, scarlet runner bean (*Phaseolus coccineus*) has the added bonus of edible beans. Other popular annual vines include cup-and-saucer vine (*Cobaea scandens*), hyacinth bean (*Dolichos lablab*), and black-eyed Susan vine (*Thunbergia alata*). The "Guide to Annuals," starting on page 58, offers complete growing information for these easy-care annual vines.

Need a screen to block a view until you can put in a hedge or fence? Try tall annuals or biennials, such as foxglove (*Digitalis purpurea*).

A silver-and-white garden looks crisp and clean during the day. The light colors stand out at night, too.

As you plan your color theme plantings, don't forget to consider colorful leaves, such as those of coleus.

Annuals for Color Theme Gardens

There's no denying that we all have a favorite color or two. So why not indulge yourself and plant a whole garden dedicated to your most cherished colors? Annual displays designed around a particular color are fun to plan, and the results can be delightful.

Color Considerations

If you're not sure exactly which color to choose, think about the time of day you'll usually view the garden and what kind of weather prevails in your area. If your climate tends to be cloudy and misty, whites, yellows, and pastels can be useful for adding a bright touch to your yard. White flowers also tend to glow luminously in twilight or moonlit gardens. If sun shines down on your garden for most of the season, consider bright colors for your theme.

Themes to Try

Unless you're trying to create a specific landscape effect, the colors you choose to highlight in your garden are really a matter of personal taste. You may want to be restrained and stick to different tints and shades of the same color—all yellows or pinks, for instance. Or you may enjoy expanding your palette a bit and grouping two or more colors.

Hot Color Borders If knock-your-socks-off color is what you want, consider planning a garden around the hot colors: reds, oranges, and yellows. These colors are ideal for accenting outlying areas of your yard, since

they tend to catch your eye across long distances. Many annuals are available in these bright hues.

Cool Color Borders If you're not especially adventurous in your color choices, a planting of cool colors may be more to your liking. Blues, violets, and greens are best planted where you can see them up

Don't Forget Foliage

As you experiment with different annual combinations, remember that flowers aren't the only source of color; leaves have lots to offer, too. They come in a surprising array of different greens, from the blue-green of California poppy (*Eschscholzia californica*) to the yellow-green of summer cypress (*Kochia scoparia*) or the deep green of geraniums. Fortunately, nearly all greens are agreeable colors that go well together and set off most flowers.

Besides the various greens, leaves can come in other colors, too. Silver-leaved plants such as dusty miller look great in almost any kind of garden. Yellowish leaves, such as those of golden feverfew or some coleus, can be pleasing with pinks and blues. You can add a bold spire of color with the blazing red leaves of Joseph's coat (*Amaranthus tricolor*) or a subtle accent with the bronzy leaves of wax begonias. As you select annuals for your garden, try to include a few with interesting foliage to add extra color and season-long interest.

If you're looking for can't-miss color, an all-red border might be the perfect accent for your yard.

Blues and purples look best where you can see them up close. From a distance, they'll blend into the background.

close—perhaps along a path or near a deck. If you plant these deep colors in distant beds, they'll tend to fade into the background.

Wonderful White Gardens A white garden is an elegant addition to any yard. There's just nothing like crisp whites for brightening up dull areas. And white plantings are also nice at night, when they will reflect the light from the moon or nearby streetlamps.

Many common annuals that are available in a range of colors—including petunias, cosmos, and cleome

(*Cleome hasslerana*)—are available in white as well. Choose cultivars that have been selected for white flowers, or buy plants in bloom to make sure they are white.

Pretty Pastel Plantings Like cool color plantings, soft pinks, yellows, and baby blues planted together tend to have a calm, soothing look. To keep the garden from looking too washed out, consider adding a little spark with some bright whites or a deeper hue of one of the colors—perhaps pure yellow marigolds or bright pink verbena (*Verbena* x *hybrida*).

Annuals for an All-blue Garden

Blue theme gardens have a cool, restrained look, but they're tricky to pull off successfully. Blue and green are such similar colors that blue flowers tend to blend into the background sea of green leaves.

Varying the different kinds of blue— from soft lavender-blue to bright sky blue and deep cobalt blue—is one way to add extra interest to a cool-color planting. Companion plants with silver or chartreuse leaves, such as dusty miller or golden feverfew (*Chrysanthemum parthenium* 'Aureum'), are also excellent additions for contrast.

The following list contains a few blue-flowered annuals you might want to include in your cool color garden. For more information on growing these annuals, see their entries in the "Guide to Annuals," starting on page 58.

Ageratum houstonianum (ageratum)
Brachycome iberidifolia (Swan River daisy)
Browallia speciosa (browallia)
Centaurea cyanus (cornflower)
Consolida ambigua (rocket larkspur)
Convolvulus tricolor (dwarf morning glory)
Ipomoea tricolor (morning glory)
Lobelia erinus (edging lobelia)
Myosotis sylvatica (forget-me-not)
Nemophila menziesii (baby-blue-eyes)
Nigella damascena (love-in-a-mist)
Salvia farinacea (mealy-cup sage)

Annuals for Cutting Gardens

If you enjoy having fresh cut flowers to display indoors but dislike denuding your carefully planned flower beds, consider starting a cutting garden. It doesn't need to be anything fancy. It could be part of an existing vegetable or herb garden or any place with at least a half-day of sun, an accessible water source, and average, workable soil. A few rows of annuals for cutting can provide a generous supply of fresh flowers for much of the growing season.

Create Your Own Cutting Garden

If you already have a garden area where other plants grow well, the conditions are probably ideal for a cutting garden. If you're converting an existing lawn area, you'll need to strip off the sod and dig in some compost to loosen and enrich the soil. (You'll find complete details on starting a garden from scratch in "Preparing the Soil and Planting" on page 49.)

Sow annual seeds or set out

Plant flowers for cutting in rows for easy picking.

Strawflowers are great for cutting gardens, since you can use them in either fresh or dried arrangements.

transplants just as you would for any garden, but don't worry about grouping specific heights and colors; just plant them in rows. Mulch between the rows with a loose organic material (such as straw) to discourage weeds, keep the soil moist, and prevent soil from splashing up on the flowers. Water as needed to keep the soil evenly moist for best growth.

Handling Cut Flowers

The best time to collect cut flowers is in the morning, before it gets too hot. Select blooms that are just

---

Best Bets for Cutting

As you decide which annuals you'll grow for cutting, keep in mind that some thrive in the heat of summer while others prefer cooler temperatures. Plan to sow some each of early-, mid-, and late-summer flowers to have a steady supply of blooms.

Following is a list of some suitable annuals for cut flowers, along with their normal peak bloom season. For complete growing information, see the individual entries in the "Guide to Annuals," starting on page 58.

Antirrhinum majus (snapdragon; midsummer)

Calendula officinalis (pot marigold; early summer)

Callistephus chinensis (China aster; midsummer)

Celosia cristata (celosia; late summer)

Centaurea cyanus (cornflower; midsummer)

Consolida ambigua (rocket larkspur; midsummer)

Cosmos bipinnatus (cosmos; late summer)

Cosmos sulphureus (yellow cosmos; midsummer)

Dianthus barbatus (sweet William; early summer)

Gaillardia pulchella (blanket flower; midsummer)

Gypsophila elegans (annual baby's-breath; early summer)

Helianthus annuus (common sunflower; late summer)

Iberis umbellata (annual candytuft; early summer)

Lathyrus odoratus (sweet pea; early summer)

Matthiola incana (stock; early summer)

Rudbeckia hirta (black-eyed Susan; midsummer)

Tithonia rotundifolia (Mexican sunflower; late summer)

Viola x *wittrockiana* (pansy; early summer)

Zinnia elegans (zinnia; midsummer)

The bright flowers and ferny foliage of cosmos are excellent additions to fresh arrangements in late summer.

opening. Cut the bloom stalks with shears or a sharp knife, taking as much stem as you think you'll need for your arrangement. Gather some foliage to use as a filler and a backdrop for the flowers. Put cut stems immediately into a pail of lukewarm water.

When you are finished cutting, take your flowers indoors and pull the leaves off the bottom part of the stems. You can arrange your flowers right away or return the stems to the pail of water and set them in a cool, dark place overnight until you're ready for them.

Before arranging flowers and foliage, remove the leaves from the bottom half of the stem.

If you don't want to set aside an area just for cut flowers, you can snip blooms from beds and borders as needed.

Sunflowers are ideal for fresh arrangements. Grow a variety of sizes and colors so you'll have an ample supply.

Annuals for Fragrance

To some gardeners, having fragrant flowers is just as important as having particular colors or kinds of plants. If you're a fragrance fanatic, there are some wonderfully scented annuals that you just shouldn't be without.

Scented Blooms

For fragrant flowers, consider sweet William (*Dianthus barbatus*) or China pinks (*D. chinensis*), two carnation relatives noted for their spicy scents. Sweet alyssum (*Lobularia maritima*) is a common and easy-to-grow annual that's beloved for its fresh, honey-like fragrance. Mignonette (*Reseda odorata*) is an old-fashioned favorite with small, insignificant flowers but a powerful and delightful fragrance.

A few annuals withhold their scents until the sun sets, then release their sweet perfume on the evening breeze. Night-scented stock (*Matthiola longipetala* subsp. *bicornis*), sweet rocket (*Hesperis matronalis*), and flowering tobacco (*Nicotiana sylvestris*) carry remarkably potent night scents.

Stock has a rich, spicy fragrance that is noticeable in the garden or in fresh arrangements indoors.

Fragrant Foliage

Of course, flowers aren't the only source of garden scents; some annuals have fragrant leaves as well. Scented geraniums (including *Pelargonium tomentosum, P. crispum,* and *P. graveolens*) are noted for their aromatic leaves. When you rub them, they release scents resembling those of peppermint, lemons, roses, and many other plants. Annual herbs such as basil, anise, and dill also offer fragrant foliage; see "Annuals for Herb Gardens" on page 41 for more information on these spicy-scented favorites.

Gardening with Fragrance

To get the most pleasure from your fragrant plants, grow them where you will walk, sit, or brush by them often. Try them along the path to your front door, around a deck or patio, or in a foundation planting near open windows for indoor enjoyment. Raised beds and container gardens are especially good spots for scented plants, since they'll be closer to your nose and easier to sniff.

Favorite Fragrant Annuals

Here is a list of a few easy annuals and biennials that are commonly grown for their fragrance. Keep in mind that scents are subjective; what's pleasing to one person may be undetectable or offensive to another. If possible, try to sniff plants before you buy them to see if you like the fragrance. For complete growing information, see the individual entries in the "Guide to Annuals," starting on page 58.

Cheiranthus cheiri (wallflower)
Dianthus barbatus (sweet William)
Dianthus chinensis (China pink)
Heliotropium arborescens (common heliotrope)
Ipomoea alba (moonflower)
Lathyrus odoratus (sweet pea)
Lobularia maritima (sweet alyssum)
Matthiola incana (stock)
Mirabilis jalapa (four-o'clock)
Nicotiana alata (flowering tobacco)
Petunia x *hybrida* (petunia)
Tagetes hybrids (marigolds)

Not all flowering tobacco cultivars are scented. Sniff the blooms before you buy if fragrance is important to you.

Parsley has rich green leaves and a nice clumping habit that make it an attractive companion for flowers.

Create a colorful and practical planting by mixing herbs with annual flowers, such as pot marigold (*Calendula officinalis*).

Annuals for Herb Gardens

Besides adding colorful flowers and handsome foliage to your garden, some annuals can even add flavor to your food! Annual herbs are easy to grow, and they'll produce generous quantities of tasty leaves or seeds to spice up your favorite dishes.

As with other annuals, annual herbs are quite useful for filling the gaps around new perennial plantings. If you have a formal herb garden with traditional perennial herbs, such as sage, thyme, and mint, scatter seed of annual herbs among the young plants. Or use the annual herbs throughout your yard as you would any other filler annual, and you'll have flower beds that are productive as well as beautiful.

Easy Annual Herbs

If you enjoy cooking with herbs, annuals provide lots of scope for experimentation. Some commonly grown annual herbs include anise, basil, borage, chervil, coriander, dill, and parsley. Here are some details on a few of the most popular annual herbs.

Basil What would a cook's garden be without basil? This peppery herb is a traditional part of pestos and tomato dishes. It's also a snappy addition to salads, poultry, pasta, rice, eggs, and vegetable dishes. For best growth, give basil a site with full sun and rich, well-drained soil. Sow seeds of this heat-loving herb directly into the garden in late spring, or set out transplants after all danger of frost has passed. Snip the leaves as needed. For extra interest, look for purple-leaved basil cultivars; they are ornamental as well as edible.

Coriander Actually, coriander is the name commonly used for the seeds of *Coriandrum sativum,* while the leaves are often referred to as cilantro. The leaves have a powerful odor and a flavor that combines sage and citrus. The fresh leaves and roots are popular in many cuisines for use in salads, sauces, and relishes. The citrus-flavored seeds are a nice addition to herbal teas or desserts. Sow the seed outdoors in spring in a spot with sun to light shade and rich, well-drained soil. Sow again every 2 to 3 weeks until late summer for a continuous supply of fresh leaves. Pick the leaves as needed; harvest the seeds when they begin to fall from the flower heads.

Dill Grow dill for its lacy green leaves and flavorful seeds. The fresh leaves (often called "dill weed") are a popular addition to fish dishes, as well as vegetable dishes, sauces, and salads. Dill seed is most commonly used as a pickling spice. Sow the seed outdoors in spring in full sun and rich, well-drained soil. Snip the leaves as needed; collect the seeds when they turn brown and begin to drop.

Parsley Both the curly-leaved and flat-leaved types of parsley are edible, but the flat-leaved type has the best flavor. Parsley goes with just about any kind of food except desserts. Mix minced parsley into butter or margarine for a flavorful spread, or add chopped parsley to salsa. In the garden, parsley forms attractive clumps that make a nice edging for a flower garden. Sow seed directly into the garden in early spring, or set out transplants. Snip the outer leaves as needed. Parsley is actually a biennial; it will flower and produce seeds (but few leaves) during the second year.

GROWING ANNUALS

With some basic care, annuals and biennials can provide a long season of color and beauty. Whether you buy them as plants from your local garden center or start your own transplants from seed, annuals and biennials are a fairly inexpensive way to fill your garden with flowers. And when you provide a good growing site, plant them properly, and give them a little routine maintenance, their beautiful blooms will give you a big return for your money.

In this chapter, you'll learn all the down-and-dirty details you need to know to have a healthy, gorgeous garden all season long. If you enjoy raising your plants from seed, check out "Growing Annuals from Seed" on page 44. You'll find great tips here on deciding whether to sow indoors in pots or outdoors in the garden. Hints on how to protect your seedlings from disease will also help you get great results.

If you don't have the time or room to grow your own annuals from seed, purchasing transplants from a garden center or nursery is the way to go. In "Buying Healthy Transplants" on page 48, you'll learn the secrets to picking out the plants that are most likely to thrive when you get them home.

Starting with strong healthy seedlings is a major part of successful gardening, but it won't do you any good if you don't plant them properly. "Preparing the Soil and Planting" on page 49 explains how to start a new garden from scratch, dig the soil, and set out transplants. It also tells how to protect your little plants from frost and pests so they can get the best possible start in life.

Throughout the season, a little care will keep your annuals and biennials looking their best. "Caring for Annuals" on page 52 explains the basics of mulching, weeding, watering, staking, pinching, deadheading, and fall garden cleanup. You'll also find out how to collect seeds for next year's garden and how to bring annuals indoors for winter color.

While good care goes a long way toward keeping your annuals and biennials at their peak, insects and diseases can sometimes damage the flower display. In "Handling Pest and Disease Problems" on page 56, you'll learn how to prevent problems from starting and how to use safe, effective, organic controls to deal with the ones that do occur.

At the end of this chapter, you'll find the "Guide to Annuals," starting on page 58. Each entry has a color photograph to show you what the plant looks like, as well as a description, the height and spread, best site, growing guidelines, and suggested landscape uses. Skim through the entries to find plants that you'd like to try, or look up specific plants you have in mind to find out how to care for them.

Knowing what conditions your plants need will help you choose the best planting site and provide the best care. Sweet peas (*Lathyrus odoratus*), for instance, need rich soil, lots of sun and moisture, and a support to climb.

lids, plastic bags, or plastic food wrap will help to keep the mix moist and reduce or eliminate the need to water. (This is especially important for small, surface-sown seeds, since they can dry out quickly.) Most seeds sprout in 1 to 3 weeks. Remove the glass or plastic covering as soon as you see seedlings appear.

Growing Healthy Seedlings Once your seedlings are up, move them to full light (if they're not there already). Place them on a sunny windowsill or under the lights you've set up. Hang the lights so they're about 4 inches (10 cm) above the seedlings. Keep the lights on 14 to 16 hours a day. An inexpensive timer can turn the lights on and off for you automatically.

Seedling pots tend to dry out quickly indoors. Water them every few days to keep the soil evenly moist. If possible, water them from the bottom by adding about $^1/_2$ inch (12 mm) of water to the tray the pots are sitting in. (Do not let the pots sit in water continuously.) Watering carefully from the top is also an option.

When your seedlings have produced two sets of true

Some annuals, including strawflowers (*Helichrysum bracteatum*), grow equally well when started indoors or out.

leaves—the ones that appear after the first "seed" leaves—they're ready to be transplanted to individual pots or cell packs. Fill the pots with moistened potting mix. Use a knife blade or the pointed end of a plant label to dig small clumps of seedlings out of the tray. Gently separate the seedlings, holding them by their leaves (not their fragile stems). Make a depression in the new pot, lower the seedling roots into the hole, and carefully fill around the roots with potting mix.

Set planted pots in a shallow tray of water until the soil surface looks moist. Shade them from full sun and keep them cool for a day or two before moving them back to the windowsill or their spot under lights. Keep the soil evenly moist. Periodically apply a dose of liquid fertilizer (such as fish emulsion), following the manufacturer's directions for seedlings.

Sowing Seed in the Garden

If you don't have the time or space to raise seedlings indoors, you can still grow a wide variety of annuals from seed. Many popular annuals grow just as well from seed sown outdoors as from seed sown indoors. Some even grow *better* from direct-sown seed because they prefer cool outdoor temperatures or because they don't respond well to transplanting. A few annuals in this easy-to-grow group include morning glories (*Ipomoea* spp.), California poppy (*Eschscholzia californica*), and rocket larkspur (*Consolida ambigua*). To find out if the annuals you want to grow can be direct-sown, check the seed packet or the entries in the "Guide to Annuals," starting on page 58. These sources will also tell you the best time for sowing.

Dealing with Damping-off

Damping-off is a disease that can strike young seedlings, killing them just before or after they emerge. Affected seedlings tend to topple over, since their stems are damaged at the soil level. Once a few seedlings are affected, the disease can quickly spread to other seedlings in the same pot or tray.

Since there's no real cure, the best way to handle damping-off is prevention. Here are some tips to consider; try one or all!

- Always use fresh, "sterile" seed-starting mix.
- If you're reusing old pots or trays, knock out the old soil, dip the containers in a 10 percent bleach solution (1 part household bleach to 9 parts water), and let the containers dry before using them.
- Sprinkle a thin layer of milled sphagnum moss on top of newly planted seeds.
- Improve air circulation with a small fan set to blow lightly just over the tops of the seedlings.
- If damping-off strikes outdoor-sown seeds, wait until the weather warms up (maybe 2 to 3 weeks), then try sowing again.

Impatiens are sensitive to cold, so it's best to start them indoors and set them out after the last frost date.

Direct-sowing is simple. First, get the soil ready for planting (as explained in "Preparing the Soil and Planting" on page 49). Sow medium-sized and large seeds individually or scatter them evenly over the surface. Try to space them ¹/₂ to 1 inch (12 to 25 mm) apart. If you have very small seeds, mix them with a handful of dry sand and distribute them over the seedbed.

Cover most seeds with a thin layer of fine soil or sand. If you're dealing with fine seeds, just pat them into the soil or tamp down the area with a board. After sowing, make sure the seedbed stays moist until the seedlings are visible. If rainfall is lacking, water gently with a watering can, sprinkler, or fine hose spray. Covering the seedbed with a layer of floating row cover

Nursery Beds for Biennials

If you decide to grow biennial plants, such as foxgloves (*Digitalis purpurea*) and forget-me-nots (*Myosotis sylvatica*), you need a slightly different growing approach. Most biennials will sprout well when sown outdoors, so that part is easy. But if you sow them directly into the garden, their leafy, first-year growth will take up room without adding much interest to your flower display.

The easiest approach is to set aside a temporary growing area (called a nursery bed) where your biennials can grow through the summer. Prepare your nursery bed just as you would any garden area, but site it in an out-of-the-way spot. Sow the biennial seeds into the bed in spring or summer, and thin them as needed. Dig the plants and move them to their final garden spots in late summer or early fall for bloom the following spring or summer.

helps to keep the soil moist and protects the seed from drying winds, heavy rain, and birds. (Remove the cover once the seedlings emerge.)

If seedlings are crowded, you'll need to thin them out for good growth. Dig up and carefully transplant extra seedlings, or use scissors to cut off the stems of unwanted seedlings at ground level.

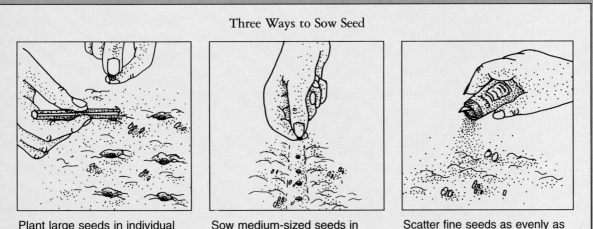

Three Ways to Sow Seed

Plant large seeds in individual holes, or cover them with a layer of soil.

Sow medium-sized seeds in shallow rows, and cover them lightly with soil.

Scatter fine seeds as evenly as you can over the surface of the soil; press them in lightly.

Buying Healthy Transplants

Who can resist the parade of brilliant blossoms for sale at every garden center each spring? It's sometimes difficult to be a smart shopper when faced with such floral extravagance. The key is to look beyond the flowers and make a close inspection of the plants themselves.

Smart Shopping Strategies

When you shop, look for plants that are fairly uniform and seem healthy. Avoid those that are wilted, as well as those with visible problems. (See the "Healthy Plant Checklist" for signs and symptoms to look for.) While wilted plants usually recover when watered, repeated wilting can stunt their growth and make them less likely to perform well in your garden over the season.

Another thing to consider is whether or not the plants are in bloom. If you're looking for specific flower colors, you may want to buy plants that already have some blooms. In most cases, though, you'll get the best growth from plants that aren't yet blooming.

If you're looking for particular colors, buy plants that have a few blooms. Otherwise, try to find plants that aren't flowering yet.

If you can only buy transplants that are already flowering, pinch off the flowers at planting time. It seems hard to do, but it will help your plants in the long run. They'll put their energy into making new roots and then quickly start producing bushy new growth and dozens of new flower buds.

Healthy Plant Checklist

In the fun and frenzy of spring plant shopping, it's easy to overlook quality in the quest for getting the "perfect" plant. But as you choose, keep in mind that bringing home a stressed, diseased, or pest-infested plant is a recipe for disappointing results. Before you pay for your purchases, take a minute to check them over carefully—following the points here—to make sure you're getting the best plants possible.

1. Peruse the plant. It should be similar in size and color to other plants of the same type. Avoid plants that seem stunted or off-color.

2. Look at the leaves. Avoid plants with yellowed leaves or brown tips (signs of improper watering). Carefully turn over a few leaves and check the undersides for signs of pests.

Avoid plants with tiny white insects that fly up when you move the leaves (whiteflies); clusters of small, pear-shaped insects (aphids); or yellow-stippled leaves with tiny webs underneath (caused by spider mites).

3. Check the stems. They should be stocky and evenly colored, with no visible cuts, bruises, or pest problems.

4. Inspect the roots. It's okay if a few roots are coming out of the drainage holes at the bottom of the pot, but masses of tangled roots indicate that the plant is long overdue for transplanting. Overgrown plants can be saved if you loosen or remove some of the matted roots at transplanting time, but it's better to start with younger plants if you have a choice.

Preparing the Soil and Planting

Buying or raising healthy transplants is one secret of starting a healthy garden; preparing a good growing area is the other. In this section, you'll learn all the basics of creating an ideal growing site, planting your annuals properly, and protecting them so they get off to the best start possible.

If you're going to tuck transplants in around existing plants in beds and borders, you can simply dig an individual hole for each transplant.

Starting from Scratch

If you've just moved into a new house, you have the luxury of laying out your landscape before doing any planting. Mark off the areas you want for flower gardens, install the trees, shrubs, and lawns in the other areas, then skip down to "Getting Ready to Plant" to learn how to dig the flower beds for planting.

For most of us, though, new flower gardens must be reclaimed from existing lawn areas. You have two options for removing the existing sod—by hand or machine.

Removing Sod by Hand Digging up sod by hand is an option if you have plenty of time and energy or if you have only a small area to clear. Water the area a day or two before, then use a spade to cut the sod into small squares, about 6 inches (15 cm) on each side. Pull up each block (slide the spade under it if it doesn't come up easily), and shake it over the bed to remove excess soil. Then toss the block in a wheelbarrow to go to your compost pile.

Using a Sod-cutting Machine Renting a sod-cutting machine is the quickest and easiest way to clear large areas for planting. The blade cuts easily through moistened soil, severing the grass roots 1 to 2 inches (2.5 to 5 cm) below the soil surface. The resulting sod strips are easy to roll up (just don't make them too big, since they can be quite heavy!). Compost the sod pieces or use them to patch worn areas of your lawn.

Once the sod is gone, rake the area thoroughly to remove stray tufts of grass and roots. These pieces are easy to overlook, but they can resprout later and spread throughout the bed. This is also a good time to install some kind of plastic or metal edging strip around the outside of the planting area to keep adjacent lawn areas from creeping back into the bed.

Getting Ready to Plant

Once you have a site with bare soil, you're ready to start digging. Digging will loosen the soil and work in any needed amendments.

The ideal time to prepare a planting area is in fall. This will give the amendments a chance to improve the soil conditions and allow the soil to settle. If you don't get around to preparing the planting area in fall, then early spring is okay, too. You can dig as soon as the soil thaws, as long as it isn't too wet. (If you squeeze a handful of soil and it stays in a lump when touched lightly, the soil is too wet.) Digging wet soil

Once you remove the sod, dig or till the area to loosen the soil.

Rake the area smooth, then use a stick to mark a planting pattern.

Set out your transplants, making sure you space them evenly.

can damage its good, crumbly structure and create poor conditions for root growth.

Adding Amendments In "Soil and Site Conditions" on page 23, you learned how to tell if your soil is sandy, loamy, or clayey. Loamy soil tends to be ideal for growing a wide range of annual flowers. Sandy soil is usually dry and infertile, while clay tends to be soggy when wet and hard as a rock when dry. Unless you're growing plants that prefer fairly lean conditions (like nasturtiums [*Tropaeolum majus*]), you'll want to work some organic matter into the soil. Organic matter helps sand hold more water, loosens heavy clay, and adds a slow-release supply of nutrients to all soils.

If you already have a compost pile, you have a great source of organic matter for your flower garden. If you don't have compost or if you don't have enough, check to see if your community has a composting program; you may be able to get all you need at no charge. You can also buy bags of composted manure at most garden and home centers, or check your Yellow Pages for commercial compost suppliers. You'll need enough compost to spread a 1- to 3-inch (2.5 to 7.5 cm) thick layer over the soil.

Dusty millers are popular for their silvery leaves. They adapt well to different soils as long as the drainage is good.

Digging In Unlike perennial flowers, which benefit from deep digging, most annuals are relatively shallow-rooted. Loosening the top 8 to 10 inches (20 to 25 cm) of soil will provide good conditions for root growth. Use a spade or shovel to turn the top soil layer, working in any compost you've added. A rotary tiller can be useful if you have a large area to prepare.

After loosening the soil, rake the surface to smooth it and break up any large clods. Then let the bed soil settle for several weeks before planting. One more raking just before planting will provide a smooth surface for sowing seeds (as explained in "Sowing Seed in the Garden" on page 24).

Setting Out Transplants

You have your plants, and you have a place to put them. Now you're nearly ready to plant. The last step is to make sure your seedlings are "hardened off"—adjusted to outdoor conditions—before setting them out in the garden. For details on this important step, see "Handling Hardening Off."

When actually planting your annuals, refer back to the notes you made earlier in the season. (See "Planning Your Plantings" on page 24 for details.) Those notes will remind you where you wanted the different plants to go and what spacings they need. You can also check back to the seed packets, plant labels, or entries in the "Guide to Annuals,"

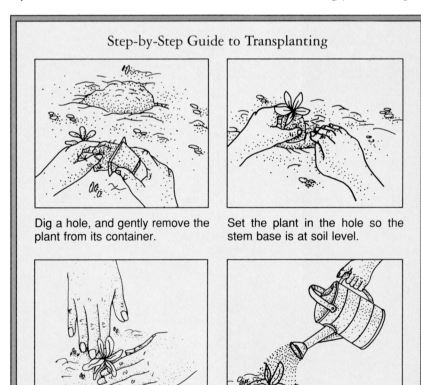

Step-by-Step Guide to Transplanting

Dig a hole, and gently remove the plant from its container.

Set the plant in the hole so the stem base is at soil level.

Gently firm the soil around the base of the plant.

Water each plant thoroughly to moisten the soil around the roots.

Gloriosa daisies (*Rudbeckia hirta*) grow fine in average soil; you don't need to add lots of extra compost.

Handling Hardening Off

If you buy greenhouse-grown seedlings or raise your own indoors, they will need to be hardened off before transplanting. This involves gradually exposing them to the harsher outdoor conditions: more sunlight, drying winds, and varying temperatures.

Start by moving seedlings outdoors on a nice day. Set shade-loving annuals in a sheltered, shady spot for 2 or 3 days before planting. Give sun-loving annuals about 1 hour of full sun, then move them into the shade of a fence or covered porch. (Take them in at night if frost threatens.) Lengthen the sun time each day, over a period of at least 3 days, until plants can take a full day of sun. Then you can plant them in the garden.

If you don't have a shady spot or if you work during the day and can't run home to shift flats of annuals, make a simple shelter with a section of lath fencing (sometimes called snow fencing). Support the section with bricks or blocks and slide your seedlings underneath. The laths will give a continuously shifting pattern of sun and shade. After 3 or 4 days, your seedlings should be in ideal condition for transplanting.

starting on page 58, for suggested spacing information. If you live in a hot, dry climate or an area with a short growing season, you may want to set plants a little closer together so they'll shade the soil and fill in faster. In humid climates, use the suggested or slightly wider spacings to allow good air circulation between plants and to minimize disease problems.

To set out plants, use a trowel to dig a hole twice as big as the root mass. Tip the pot or cell pack on its side, and gently slide the plant out of its container. Or, if the plant is growing in a peat pot, just tear off the upper rim of the pot and place the whole pot in the hole. Set each plant so the stem base is at the same level as it was in the pot. Fill around the roots with soil, firm the soil gently, and water thoroughly.

Protecting Young Plants

If temperatures are unseasonably warm, your transplants may appreciate a few days of sun protection, especially during the afternoon. Use the lath fencing you used for hardening them off (see "Handling Hardening Off" for details), or shelter them with sheets of newspaper clipped to stakes or cages. Mist seedlings occasionally if they wilt, but don't add

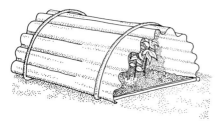

Row covers can be handy for protecting tender seedlings from frost.

a lot of extra water to the soil; swampy soil is as bad as dry soil for tender roots.

If late frosts threaten, protect plants through the night with overturned cans, buckets, or clay flower pots. Floating row covers (weigh down the edges with rocks or boards) can provide a few degrees of frost protection and also protect young plants from birds and animal pests.

Sometimes soil-dwelling caterpillars called cutworms will feed on seedlings at night, eating them off right at ground level. Once cutworms strike, the plant is gone. To protect young plants, you can surround them with a metal or cardboard collar. Slip sections of paper towel rolls over seedlings or open-ended soup or juice cans over transplants. Press the collar into the soil, so at least 1 inch (2.5 cm) is below the soil and several inches are left above. Remove metal collars after 2 to 3 weeks, or mulch over them and remove them at the end of the season; paper collars will break down on their own.

Caring for Annuals

While most annuals can grow just fine without much help from you, providing some basic care through the season will keep your plants looking their best.

Mulching

Using organic mulches around your flowers is the number-one way to keep other garden maintenance to a minimum. Organic mulches—such as grass clippings, compost, chopped leaves, cocoa shells, or shredded bark—help to keep the soil moist, so plants don't need watering as often. Mulch also prevents light from reaching the soil, so weeds are less likely to sprout. And as they break down, organic mulches add a small but steady supply of nutrients and humus to the soil.

Wait until early summer to mulch your garden, when the soil has had a chance to warm up and your seedlings or transplants are at least 4 inches (10 cm) tall. Then apply a 1- to 2-inch (2.5 to 5 cm) layer of mulch over the soil. Keep the mulch at least 1 inch (2.5 cm) from the base of the stems. As the mulch breaks down, add more once or twice during the summer to keep it at the right depth. You can till or dig the mulch into the soil at the end of the season.

Give long-season annuals a boost by adding fertilizer or compost several times a season.

Don't forget that potted plants can benefit from mulch, too. Use enough to cover the soil early in the season.

Weeding

Controlling weeds is part of caring for any garden. Since the soil in annual gardens gets turned every year, perennial weeds such as dandelions and thistles usually don't have much chance to get established. But digging the soil does bring up buried weed seeds, so annual weeds can be a problem. To catch problems early, try preparing the soil for planting and letting it sit for a week or two; then hoe out any sprouting weeds before planting your annuals. Hoe or hand weed around the plants again in early summer, then mulch. After that, check beds every week or two, and hand pull any weeds that pop through the mulch.

Saving Annual Seeds

Collecting and saving seed is a fun and easy way to preserve some of your favorite annuals (and save a bit of money, too!). You'll get the best results if you stick with seeds of nonhybrid annuals. These seeds are likely to produce plants that resemble their parents. Seeds from hybrid plants—those specially bred or selected for special traits, such as color or flower form—often produce seedlings that look quite different. (You can usually tell if a plant is a hybrid by the name or the description on the seed packet or plant tag: Look for the word "hybrid" or the symbol "F1.")

Seeds of spring-blooming annuals and biennials usually are ready by midsummer; later-blooming annuals can mature their seeds through the first few frosts. On a dry day, gather seeds from seedpods that are dry and brittle but not yet open. Daisy-family plants such as marigolds and black-eyed Susans produce their seeds directly at the stem tips; simply pull or brush these off the seed head into your hand. Store harvested seed in paper envelopes in a cool, dry, mouse-proof place over the winter, until you're ready to start them in spring; then sow them as you would purchased seed.

Remove weeds as soon as you spot them to keep them from reseeding and spreading.

Forget-me-nots (*Myosotis* spp.) can reseed prolifically. If you don't want to deal with seedlings, shear off the developing seed heads.

Watering

The easiest way to handle watering is to not do it at all. If summer rains are unreliable in your area, consider sticking with annuals that are naturally adapted to somewhat dry conditions. Choosing appropriate plants and maintaining soil moisture with mulch will go a long way toward reducing or eliminating watering chores.

Of course, ignoring watering altogether isn't always a realistic option. Sometimes you really want to grow a plant that needs more water than regular rainfall can provide. Even if you select plants that can take dry conditions, they still may need some watering during prolonged dry spells. And any plants growing in containers—such as pots, window boxes and hanging baskets—will almost always need extra water.

For container gardens, hand watering—either with a hose or a watering can—is the most realistic irrigation option. Container gardens dry out quickly, so you may need to water every day (or even twice a day) during hot weather.

For plants in the ground, how often you water depends on how dry the soil is. Before you decide to water, pull back the mulch and feel the soil surface; if it's moist, wait a day or two and test again. If the surface is dry, dig a small hole with a trowel. When you see that the top 2 to 3 inches (5 to 7.5 cm) of soil are dry, it's time to water. Irrigate until the top few inches of soil are moist.

Unless your garden is very small, watering thoroughly by hand can take hours. Watering with sprinklers isn't very efficient, either, since much of the water is lost to evaporation. Plus, it wets the plant leaves, providing ideal conditions for disease development.

If you can afford a drip irrigation system, it is an easy and effective way to get water right to the soil, where the roots need it. Or, if you need a cheaper and less permanent system, try a soaker hose. This is a flattened or round hose with tiny holes that ooze water into the soil. Lay the hose evenly over the bed in spring, set your plants or sow seeds around it, and mulch over it. When you need to water, just hook up your regular garden hose to the end of the soaker hose. Turn the water on low and let it run for a few hours, until the soil is moist.

Fertilizing

Annuals grow quickly, so they need an ample supply of nutrients for good flowering. In spring, scatter a 1- to 2-inch (2.5 to 5 cm) layer of compost over the bed,

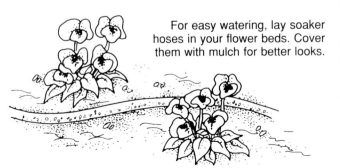

For easy watering, lay soaker hoses in your flower beds. Cover them with mulch for better looks.

To reduce watering chores, look for drought-tolerant annuals such as verbenas and black-eyed Susans (*Rudbeckia* spp.).

Working compost or organic fertilizer into the soil at planting time will supply the nutrient needs of many different annuals.

Trim climbers such as cup-and-saucer vine (*Cobaea scandens*) to direct their growth.

and dig it in as you prepare the bed for planting. Or, if you're tucking annuals around perennials and other permanent plants, mix a handful of compost into each planting hole. If you don't have compost, you could also use a general organic garden fertilizer. Once or twice during the season, pull back the mulch and scatter more compost or fertilizer around the base of each plant; then replace the mulch. For most annuals and biennials, this will provide all the nutrients they need.

For plants that appreciate extra fertility, such as wax begonias and sweet peas or for those that are looking a little tired by midsummer, a monthly dose of liquid fertilizer can provide a quick nutrient boost. Spray the leaves or water the plants with diluted fish emulsion or compost tea (made by soaking a shovelful of finished compost in a bucket of water for about a week, then straining out the soaked compost). Regular doses of liquid fertilizer (every 1 to 3 weeks) will also keep container plants healthy and vigorous.

Staking

Many annuals are bred or selected for compact growth, so staking usually isn't much of a problem. It *is* useful, though, for a few plants, such as

Insert twiggy brush around seedlings to support them as they grow.

hollyhocks, tall snapdragons, and castor beans (*Ricinus communis*). Choose stakes that are about three-quarters of the mature height of the plant. Put them in place early—before planting seed in the garden or as you set out transplants. As the plants grow, attach their stems loosely to the stake with string, twine, or plastic ties.

Shorter but thin-stemmed annuals, including love-in-a-mist (*Nigella damascena*) and rocket larkspur (*Consolida ambigua*), look awkward with individual stakes, but they benefit from some type of support. Help them stay upright by pushing short pieces of twiggy brush or branches into the soil around the plants while they're still young. The stems will grow up through and cover the brush. (If any twigs are still visible by midsummer, just snip them off with your pruning shears.)

Deadheading

Annual flowers are genetically programmed to quickly produce seed for a new generation of plants. When you pinch off spent flowers before they can form seed (a technique called deadheading), the plants will produce more flowers in an attempt to make more seed.

If your annuals have leafy stems, cut or pinch off the

Pinch off spent flowers regularly to encourage petunias, geraniums, and other annuals to bloom all season.

spent blooms or bloom stalks just above the top set of leaves. Cut leafless stems back to a main shoot or to the base of the plant. If you plan to save seed, stop dead-heading by late summer to allow some seeds to form.

Preparing for Winter

Before the first frost, take cuttings from or dig up any plants you want to take inside for the winter. Also collect any seeds you want to save.

After the first hard frost, tender and half-hardy annuals usually turn brown; pull these out and toss them in the compost pile. Hardy annuals such as alyssum and ornamental cabbages may keep blooming through several frosts; you can either pull them out in fall or wait until early spring. Foxgloves (*Digitalis purpurea*), honesty (*Lunaria annua*), and other biennials usually make it through winter just fine, but a protective layer of mulch applied after the ground is frozen can help in severe-winter areas.

Nasturtiums (*Tropaeolum majus*) prefer soil that isn't too rich, so hold off on the fertilizer for best blooms.

Bringing Annuals Indoors

The first frost of fall doesn't have to signal the end of your annuals' bloom season. With just a little effort, you can enjoy their colorful flowers on your windowsills all winter.

Tender perennials that are commonly grown as annuals usually adapt best to life indoors. These include wax begonias, geraniums (both flowering and scented-leaf types), coleus, impatiens (including New Guinea types), and heliotrope (*Heliotropium arborescens*). Overwintering these plants indoors allows you to keep them year after year, so you don't need to buy new ones each year. It's also an excellent way to preserve plants that have special traits, like especially good fragrance or a flower form or color that you particularly like.

To overwinter annuals indoors, dig up whole plants before the first fall frost, cut them back by about one-third, and plant them in pots. Or take 3- to 5-inch (7.5 to 12.5 cm) cuttings from healthy, vigorous stems in mid- to late-summer. Snip cuttings from non-flowering shoots if possible; otherwise, pinch off any flowers and flower buds. Remove the leaves from the lower half of each cutting, and insert the bottom one-third of the stem into a pot of moist potting soil. Enclose the pot in a plastic bag and set it in a bright place out of direct sun. When cuttings are well rooted— usually in 3 to 4 weeks—remove the bag and move the pot to a sunny windowsill.

Whether you bring in whole plants or just cuttings, inspect them carefully first for any signs of pests or diseases. Avoid bringing in affected plants if possible. If you really want to save a special plant that has a problem, treat it as explained in "Pests and Problems of Annuals" on page 57.

During the winter, handle your annuals as you would other houseplants. In the spring, move them back into the garden after the last frost date. Help them make the adjustment between indoors and outdoors by moving them out gradually; see "Handling Hardening Off" on page 51 for guidelines.

Healthy, vigorous plants that are not crowded are naturally less inviting to pest and disease problems.

Botrytis blight can cause a fuzzy gray mold on stems, buds, or flowers; pick off infected parts.

Handling Pest and Disease Problems

Annuals are among the most trouble-free garden plants you can grow. If you choose annuals that are suited to your growing conditions, buy healthy plants, and give them regular care, pest and disease problems seldom become serious enough to require action on your part.

Preventing Problems

Most annuals grow best when they aren't overcrowded. Crowding leads to competition for water and nutrients, so plants are weaker and prone to problems. It also interferes with air circulation and provides ideal conditions for diseases to develop.

Besides spacing plants properly, watering correctly—by wetting the soil, not the leaves—will also prevent disease problems. Ideally, use a soaker hose or irrigation system that will ooze water onto the soil, where it will go right to the roots. If you

A paper collar can protect seedlings from cutworms.

must water plants from the top, at least do it in the morning so plants will dry quickly.

Easy Organic Controls

To catch any problems that slip past your defenses, walk through your garden at least once or twice a week. Look over each planted area, and inspect at least two or three plants in each area closely. Check the upper and lower leaf surfaces, the stems, and the buds or flowers. If you notice any damage or discoloration, match the symptoms to those listed in "Pests and Problems of Annuals" to find the possible causes and solutions.

Sprays and Dusts Some-times controlling pests is as simple as spraying them with water. This can knock small pests like mites and aphids right off the plants. Pinching or cutting off infected or infested plant parts is another easy way to remove problems. If you're not squeamish, you can even handpick large pests like caterpillars, slugs, and beetles and drop them into soapy water.

A strong spray of plain water can knock aphids and mites off your plants.

If these measures aren't effective, a simple soap spray will handle many of your pest problems. You can buy commercial insecticidal soap, or you can make your own spray by mixing 1 to 3 teaspoons of liquid dish soap in 1 gallon (4 l) of water. Soap spray can injure some plants, so test it on a few leaves and wait 2 or 3 days. If you don't notice any damage, spray the whole plant (including the leaf undersides), then repeat 2 or 3 days later.

When diseases appear, pinch off the damaged leaves and spray the rest with commercial fungicidal soap, or dust every 2 weeks with sulfur. If diseases were a problem last year, try preventive measures: Spray leaves with an antitranspirant (sold in garden centers) or dust every other week with sulfur, starting in very early spring.

Pests and Problems of Annuals

In most cases, annuals are fairly free of problems. But if your plants start looking a little sickly, use the table below to figure out what might be going wrong and what you can do about it.

What You See	Possible Causes	Suggested Controls
Leaves or flowers with large, ragged holes	Slugs, snails, beetles, caterpillars	Trap slugs and snails in shallow pans of beer; handpick beetles; spray caterpillars with BT
Leaves curled, puckered, or twisted	Aphids, leafhoppers	Spray with soap solution
Leaves stippled with yellow	Spider mites	Spray with soap solution
Leaves yellow-green; growth stunted	Aster yellows	Destroy infected plants
Leaves or stems speckled or silvery	Thrips	Spray with soap solution
Leaves yellow; plant weakened; tiny white insects on undersides of leaves	Whiteflies	Spray with soap solution
Leaves black and sticky or shiny	Sooty mold fungus	Wipe leaves with damp cloth; control aphids and other pests
Leaves and stems with small, hard bumps	Scales	Gently scrape bumps off stem with a fingernail or dull knife
Leaves and stems with white, cottony clusters	Mealybugs	Spray with soap solution
Leaves with shiny or sticky coating	Aphids, scales, whiteflies, slugs, snails	Spray with soap solution; trap slugs and snails in shallow pans of beer
Leaves or shoots with white spots or patches	Powdery mildew	Pick off badly infected leaves; spray rest with fungicidal soap
Leaves or stems with orange spots	Rust	Dust every 2 weeks with sulfur; destroy badly infected plants
Leaves with brown or black spots	Plant bugs	Handpick pests
Seedlings or young plants cut off at ground level	Cutworms	No control; protect seedling stems with a cardboard collar pressed partway into the soil
Seedlings dying	Damping-off fungus	No cure; allow soil to dry somewhat before resowing; thin seedlings to reduce crowding
Leaves, stems, buds, or flowers with fuzzy gray mold	Botrytis blight	Pick off infected leaves and flowers; thin remaining plants

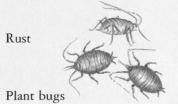

Ageratum houstonianum   Compositae

AGERATUM

Ageratums need little care; just water during dry spells. If the plants stop producing new blooms, cut them back by about half; water and fertilize to promote new growth.

OTHER COMMON NAMES: Floss flower.

DESCRIPTION: A half-hardy annual that forms tidy clumps of hairy, medium green, roughly triangular leaves. From early summer until frost, the leaves are nearly covered by clusters of ¼–½-inch (6–12 mm), puffy flower heads in shades of lavender-blue, violet-blue, pink, or white.

HEIGHT AND SPREAD: Height usually 6–12 inches (15–20 cm); spread 6–8 inches (15–20 cm).

BEST SITE: Full sun to partial shade; average, well-drained soil with some added organic matter. A site with morning sun and afternoon shade is best for plants in warm- to hot-summer climates.

GROWING GUIDELINES: Buy transplants in spring for earliest color, or start them from seed sown indoors 6–8 weeks before your last frost date. Sow seed on the surface, press it in lightly, and put the pots in plastic bags until seedlings appear. Set out young plants after the last frost. Space compact cultivars 6–8 inches (15–20 cm) apart; allow 12 inches (30 cm) between plants of tall cultivars.

LANDSCAPE USES: The compact cultivars are ideal for edging flower beds and adding color to containers. Tall-stemmed types are excellent for cut flowers and as accents in perennial borders.

CULTIVARS: 'Blue Danube' is popular for its lavender-blue color; it grows 6–8 inches (15–20 cm) tall. 'Summer Snow' has white flowers.

| *Alcea rosea* Malvaceae | *Amaranthus caudatus* Amaranthaceae |

HOLLYHOCK

LOVE-LIES-BLEEDING

Hollyhocks are perennials usually grown as annuals or biennials. Cut down the flower stalks after the blooms fade, or leave a few to set seed and self-sow.

Love-lies-bleeding is lovely in fresh or dried arrangements. To preserve the flowers, stand the cut stems in a heavy bucket so the tassels hang naturally as they dry.

DESCRIPTION: Hollyhocks form large clumps of rounded leaves and thick bloom stalks. Plump flower buds produce bowl-shaped, single or double blooms up to 5 inches (12.5 cm) wide from midsummer until fall. The crinkled petals usually bloom in white or shades of red, pink, and yellow.

HEIGHT AND SPREAD: Height 3–6 feet (90–180 cm); spread to about 2 feet (60 cm).

BEST SITE: Full sun; average, well-drained soil.

GROWING GUIDELINES: For bloom the same year, sow seed indoors 8 weeks before your last frost date. Sow ¼ inch (6 mm) deep in individual pots. After risk of frost has passed, set plants out 18–24 inches (45–60 cm) apart. For earlier bloom the following year, sow outdoors in large pots or in a nursery bed in spring or early summer. Move the young plants to their garden position in fall. Stake hollyhocks growing in exposed sites to keep stems upright. Hollyhocks are prone to rust, a fungal disease that produces orange spots on leaves. If rust shows up in your garden, pull plants out after bloom.

LANDSCAPE USES: Use the tall spires of hollyhocks as accents in a flower border, with shrubs, or along a wall or fence.

CULTIVARS: 'Summer Carnival' has double flowers in a range of colors on 5-foot (1.5 m) tall stems. 'Nigra' grows 5 feet (1.5 m) tall and has deep maroon blooms.

DESCRIPTION: This unusual tender annual produces thick, sturdy, branched stems with large, oval, pale green leaves. Long clusters of tightly packed, deep crimson flowers dangle from the stem tips from midsummer until frost. The ropy, tassel-like clusters can grow to 18 inches (45 cm) long.

HEIGHT AND SPREAD: Height 3–5 feet (90–150 cm); spread to about 2 feet (60 cm).

BEST SITE: Full sun; average, well-drained to dry soil.

GROWING GUIDELINES: Sow seed indoors, ⅛ inch (3 mm) deep, 4–6 weeks before your last frost date. Set plants out 18 inches (45 cm) apart when the weather is warm, 2–3 weeks after the last frost date. Seed also germinates quickly in warm soil, so you could instead sow it in the garden in late spring.

LANDSCAPE USES: Makes a striking accent in flower beds and borders and in cottage gardens. Add a few plants to the cutting garden, too.

CULTIVARS: 'Viridis' is similar but has green flower clusters. 'Pygmy Torch' has upright, crimson clusters above purplish leaves on 18–24-inch (45–60 cm) tall stems.

OTHER SPECIES:

A. tricolor, Joseph's coat, is grown for its large, green leaves that are splashed with yellow and bright red. The sturdy, 3-foot (90 cm) tall plants make striking accents in flower borders. Grow Joseph's coat as you would love-lies-bleeding.

SNAPDRAGON

A mass planting of snapdragons makes an eye-catching landscape accent. Pinch the stem tips of dwarf types once after transplanting to promote branching.

Medium-height and tall snapdragons look great in beds and borders with other annuals and perennials. Stake tall types to keep their stems straight.

DESCRIPTION: These tender perennials are usually grown as hardy or half-hardy annuals. The plants may be low and mound-forming or tall and spiky. The slender stems carry narrow, bright green leaves and are topped with spikes of tubular flowers that resemble puckered lips. The 1½-inch (12–25 mm), velvety flowers bloom through summer in nearly every color but true blue; some have two colors in one flower.

HEIGHT AND SPREAD: Height ranges from 1 foot (30 cm) for dwarf types to 2 feet (60 cm) for intermediate types and up to 4 feet (1.2 m) for tall types. Spread ranges from 8–18 inches (20–45 cm).

BEST SITE: Full sun to light shade (especially in hot-summer areas); average, well-drained soil with added organic matter.

GROWING GUIDELINES: Buy transplants in spring, or start your own by planting seed indoors 6–8 weeks before your last frost date. Sow seed on the surface, press it in lightly, and put the pot in a plastic bag until seedlings appear; set out seedlings after the last frost date. Or sow them directly into prepared garden soil after the last frost date. Set or thin dwarf-type plants 8 inches (20 cm) apart, intermediates 10 inches (25 cm) apart, and tall types 18 inches (45 cm) apart.

Water during dry spells to keep the soil evenly moist. Pinch or cut off spent flower spikes, especially early in the season, to promote more flowers. If you leave a few spikes to set seed near the end of the season, plants may self-sow. Snapdragons can survive mild winters, especially with a protective mulch. They overwinter as leafy clumps and will start blooming in late spring to early summer in the following year.

Snapdragons are prone to rust, a fungal disease that shows up as brownish spots on leaves. Some rust-resistant cultivars are available, but even these may show some symptoms. The best prevention is to grow snapdragons as annuals and pull the plants out of the garden in fall.

LANDSCAPE USES: Snapdragons have a spiky form that makes them excellent companions for rounded flowers, like daisies. Use the low-growing cultivars in masses or as edging plants for annual beds. Tall-stemmed snapdragons are a must in the cutting garden for fresh arrangements.

CULTIVARS: 'Magic Carpet Mixed' grows only 6 inches (15 cm) tall in a range of colors. 'Royal Carpet Mixed' is a rust-resistant cultivar with bright flowers on 8-inch (20 cm) stems. 'Ruffled Super Tetra Mixed' has ruffled blooms in a range of colors on 30-inch (75 cm) stems. 'White Wonder' grows to 18 inches (45 cm) with white blooms that have a yellow throat. 'Black Prince' has crimson flowers and reddish leaves on 18-inch (45 cm) stems.

Begonia Semperflorens-Cultorum hybrid   Begoniaceae

WAX BEGONIA

Wax begonias require little or no care during the season. Pull them out after frost, or cut them back by one-third after frost and pot them up for indoor bloom in winter.

DESCRIPTION: These tender perennials are grown as tender annuals. The succulent stems bear shiny, rounded, green or reddish brown leaves. The mounded plants are covered with single or double, 1½-inch (37 mm) flowers in red, pink, or white from June until frost.

HEIGHT AND SPREAD: Height 6–8 inches (15–20 cm); spread 6–8 inches (15–20 cm).

BEST SITE: Partial shade to sun; evenly moist soil with added organic matter. Morning sun and afternoon shade is ideal in hot-summer areas. Brown-leaved types tend to be more sun- and heat-tolerant.

GROWING GUIDELINES: Wax begonias are easiest to grow from purchased transplants in spring. If you want to try raising them yourself, sow the dust-like seed at least 12 weeks before your last frost date. Don't cover the seed; just press it lightly into the soil and place the pot in a plastic bag until seedlings appear. Set transplants out after the last frost date, when temperatures stay above 50°F (10°C) at night. Space plants 6–8 inches (15–20 cm) apart.

LANDSCAPE USES: Wax begonias are ideal as edging plants for flower beds. They also look great in pots, window boxes, and hanging baskets.

CULTIVARS: The 'Cocktail' series has bronze leaves; try deep pink 'Gin' or red-flowered 'Vodka'. 'Excel Mixed' produces green- or brown-leaved plants with red, pink, or white blooms.

Bellis perennis      Compositae

ENGLISH DAISY

Pinch off the spent flower stems of English daisies at the base to prolong bloom and prevent reseeding. Pull out plants after bloom and start new ones for next year.

DESCRIPTION: These easy-to-grow, short-lived perennials are usually grown as hardy annuals or biennials. Plants form rosettes of oval, green leaves. Short, thick stems are topped with 1–2-inch (2.5–5 cm) flowers from April to June. The daisy- or pompon-like blooms may be white, pink, or red.

HEIGHT AND SPREAD: Height to 6 inches (15 cm); spread 6–8 inches (15–20 cm).

BEST SITE: Full sun to partial shade; average, well-drained soil with added organic matter.

GROWING GUIDELINES: If your area has cool summers, you can start seed indoors in midwinter and set plants out in midspring for bloom the same year. In hot-summer areas, or for earliest spring bloom elsewhere, grow English daisies as biennials. Sow seed in pots indoors or outdoors in June or July; cover lightly. Grow seedlings in pots or in a nursery bed until fall, then transplant them to the garden. Space plants 6 inches (15 cm) apart. Protect large-flowered types with a light mulch, such as straw or pine needles, over winter.

LANDSCAPE USES: English daisies are super for spring color in flower beds and window boxes. They look wonderful edging a walk, and the blooms make charming cut flowers. For extra excitement, grow English daisies with forget-me-nots (*Myosotis sylvatica*) and spring-flowering bulbs. Follow them with wax begonias or other summer annuals.

| *Brachycome iberidifolia* | Compositae | *Brassica oleracea* | Cruciferae |

SWAN RIVER DAISY

If Swan River daisy plants get floppy after the first flush of bloom, shear them back by half and water well to promote compact growth and flowers until frost.

DESCRIPTION: This half-hardy annual forms bushy mounds of thin stems and lacy, finely cut leaves. From midsummer until frost, plants bear many 1-inch (2.5 cm), rounded, daisy-like flowers in shades of blue, purple, pink, and white. The delicately scented blooms may have a black or yellow center.

HEIGHT AND SPREAD: Height to 12 inches (30 cm); spread to 18 inches (45 cm).

BEST SITE: Full sun; average, well-drained soil with added organic matter.

GROWING GUIDELINES: For earliest bloom, buy flowering plants and set them out after your last frost date. You can also start Swan River daisy from seed planted indoors or outdoors. Sow indoors 6–8 weeks before your last frost date. Scatter the seed over the surface, lightly press it into the soil, and enclose the pot in a plastic bag until seedlings appear. Set plants out after the last frost date. Or sow directly into the garden in late spring. Space plants 6–8 inches apart to form a solid, even carpet.

LANDSCAPE USES: Swan River daisy makes an unusual edging for beds and borders. Its trailing habit is ideal for window boxes and hanging baskets.

CULTIVARS: 'Blue Star' has purplish blue, black-centered flowers with spiky-looking petals. 'White Splendour' has white flowers with black centers. 'Purple Splendour' has purple blooms with yellow centers.

ORNAMENTAL CABBAGE

Ornamental cabbages add a showy accent to late-season gardens. They withstand frost and can look good until late fall or even early spring.

OTHER COMMON NAMES: Flowering cabbage.

DESCRIPTION: This biennial is grown as an annual for its rosettes of colorful fall foliage. The smooth, glossy, blue-green leaves are marked with pink, purple, cream, or white. As temperatures get cooler in fall, the leaves in the center of the rosette become much more colorful, to the point where they are only green around the edge. Ornamental kale is very similar, but its leaves are more frilly or finely cut than those of ornamental cabbage.

HEIGHT AND SPREAD: Height 12–18 inches (30–45 cm); spread to 18 inches (45 cm).

BEST SITE: Full sun to light shade; average, well-drained soil.

GROWING GUIDELINES: In hot-summer areas, sow seed indoors; elsewhere, sow outdoors in pots or a nursery bed. Plant seed ¼ inch (6 mm) deep in midsummer. Move plants to the garden in fall. Set them in holes 1 foot (30 cm) apart and deep enough to cover the stem up to the lowest set of leaves. If caterpillars damage the leaves, pick them off by hand or spray with BT.

LANDSCAPE USES: Ornamental cabbage and kale add color to fall flower beds and borders as other annuals are finishing for the season. They are also showy in containers or large window boxes.

CULTIVARS: 'Cherry Sundae Mixed' is an ornamental cabbage with white, pink, or purplish markings.

BROWALLIA

Browallia combines beautifully with other shade-lovers, such as wax begonias, hostas, and ferns. For best growth, mulch to keep the soil moist and water during dry spells.

OTHER COMMON NAMES: Sapphire flower.

DESCRIPTION: This tender perennial is usually grown as a tender annual. The bushy plants have lance-shaped, green leaves and 2-inch (5 cm) wide, starry flowers. The purple, blue, or white flowers bloom from summer until frost.

HEIGHT AND SPREAD: Height and spread usually 8–18 inches (20–45 cm), depending on the cultivar.

BEST SITE: Partial shade; average to moist soil with added organic matter.

GROWING GUIDELINES: Buy plants in spring, or start your own by planting seed indoors 8 weeks before your last frost date. Don't cover the seed; just lightly press it into the soil. Enclose the pot in a plastic bag until seedlings appear. Set plants out after the last frost. Space compact cultivars 10–12 inches (25–30 cm) apart; allow 18 inches (45 cm) between tall types. Pinch off the stem tips of young plants once or twice to promote compact, branching growth. For winter bloom, dig plants before frost, pot them up, and bring them indoors.

LANDSCAPE USES: Browallias star-shaped flowers brighten up shady beds and borders, hanging baskets, window boxes, and container gardens.

CULTIVARS: 'Blue Troll' has blue-purple blooms on compact, rounded plants to 10 inches (25 cm) tall. 'White Bell' has white flowers on bushy plants to about 8 inches (20 cm) tall.

POT MARIGOLD

After the first flush of blooms, shear off spent pot marigold flowers to promote later rebloom, or deadhead individual flowers regularly.

OTHER COMMON NAMES: Calendula.

DESCRIPTION: Easy-to-grow hardy annual. The clumps of lance-shaped, bright to pale green, aromatic leaves are topped with single or double, daisy-like flowers in orange or yellow. The yellow- or brown-centered, 2-4 inch (5-10 cm) wide flowers tend to close during cloudy weather and at night. Pot marigolds bloom from summer to fall in most areas. In hot-summer areas, grow them for late-winter to late-spring color.

HEIGHT AND SPREAD: Height usually 12–24 inches (30–60 cm); spread to 12 inches (30 cm).

BEST SITE: Full sun; average, well-drained soil.

GROWING GUIDELINES: For summer and fall bloom, sow seed indoors 6–8 weeks before your last frost date or outdoors in early to late spring. Set plants out around the last frost date. In hot-summer areas, sow seed directly into the garden in midfall for late-winter bloom. Plant seed ¼ inch (6 mm) deep. Space plants or thin seedlings to stand 8–12 inches (20–30 cm) apart. Pot marigolds may self-sow if you let some seeds form at the end of the season.

LANDSCAPE USES: Pot marigolds are sunny accents for flower beds, borders, and containers. The strong-stemmed blooms are excellent as cut flowers.

CULTIVARS: 'Touch of Red Mixed' has flowers with a maroon-red blush on the back of each petal; height to 18 inches (45 cm).

Callistephus chinensis   Compositae   *Campanula medium*   Campanulaceae

CHINA ASTER

CANTERBURY BELLS

China asters bloom from late summer to frost in white, cream, pink, red, purple, or blue. To minimize disease problems, plant them in a different spot each year.

Plan ahead for next year's flowers by starting seed during the summer, or buy overwintered container-grown plants in spring for blooms the same year.

DESCRIPTION: This tender annual is grown for its showy blooms. The stems carry broadly oval, toothed, green leaves and are topped with daisy-like or puffy, single or double flowers up to 5 inches (12.5 cm) wide.

HEIGHT AND SPREAD: Height 12–24 inches (30–60 cm); spread 12–18 inches (30–45 cm).

BEST SITE: Full sun; average, well-drained soil with added organic matter.

GROWING GUIDELINES: For late-summer bloom, buy transplants in spring or sow seed indoors, ⅛ inch (3 mm) deep, 6 weeks before your last frost date. Set plants out 1-2 weeks after the last frost date, when the weather is warm. For fall bloom, sow seed directly into the garden after the last frost date. Space plants or thin seedlings of most types to stand 10-12 inches (25-30 cm) apart; leave 18 inches (45 cm) between tall-stemmed cultivars. Pinch off stem tips once in early summer to promote branching. Stake tall cultivars. Remove spent flowers. Control aphids with soap sprays to prevent the spread of aster yellows, which causes yellowed, stunted growth; destroy infected plants. Aster wilt is a soilborne disease that causes plants to droop; destroy infected plants.

LANDSCAPE USES: Grow in masses or mix with other plants in beds, borders, and planters for late-season color. Grow a few in the cutting garden, too.

DESCRIPTION: Canterbury bells form leafy rosettes of toothed, lance-shaped leaves during their first year. In the second year, they send up slender stalks topped with loose spikes of bell-shaped blooms in white, pink, or purple-blue. The spring to early-summer flowers may be single or surrounded by a larger, colored cup.

HEIGHT AND SPREAD: Height 18–36 inches (45–90 cm); spread 12 inches (30 cm).

BEST SITE: Full sun; average, well-drained soil.

GROWING GUIDELINES: Sow seed outdoors in summer in pots or a nursery bed. Cover the seed lightly and keep the soil moist until seedlings appear. Move plants to their flowering positions in fall or early spring. Space plants 12 inches (30 cm) apart. Pinch off spent blooms to prolong flowering. Pull out plants that have finished blooming.

LANDSCAPE USES: Canterbury bells are naturals for cottage gardens. In beds and borders, grow them in small clumps with later-blooming annuals and perennials that can fill in the space left when you remove spent plants in midsummer. Try Canterbury bells in containers and cutting gardens, too.

CULTIVARS: 'Cup and Saucer Mixed' has double-cupped blooms on 30-inch (75 cm) stems. 'Russian Pink' has pink flowers on 15-inch (37.5 cm) stems; it will bloom the first year from a late-winter indoor sowing.

Catharanthus roseus   Apocynaceae

MADAGASCAR PERIWINKLE

In most areas, Madagascar periwinkle blooms from early summer until frost; it can flower nearly any time of the year in frost-free climates. Try it in pots and planters.

OTHER COMMON NAMES: Rosy periwinkle, vinca.

DESCRIPTION: A tender perennial commonly grown as a tender annual, Madagascar periwinkle forms compact, bushy clumps of glossy, dark green leaves with white central veins. Stems are topped with flat, five-petaled, white, rose, or pink flowers up to 2 inches (5 cm) wide.

HEIGHT AND SPREAD: Height and spread usually 12–18 inches (30–45 cm); larger in frost-free areas.

BEST SITE: Full sun; average, well-drained soil. Tolerates heat, pollution, and drought.

GROWING GUIDELINES: For best results, buy transplants in spring; grows slowly from seed. If you want to try raising your own, sow seed ¼ inch (6 mm) deep indoors 10–12 weeks before your last frost date. Keep pots in an especially warm place (75–80°F [24–27°C]) until seedlings appear; then move pots to regular room temperature. Set transplants out 1–2 weeks after the last frost date, when the soil is warm. Space plants 6–12 inches (15–30 cm) apart. Pinch off stem tips in early summer to promote compact growth and more flowers.

LANDSCAPE USES: This is a beautiful, easy-care annual for edging flower beds, borders, and walkways. It also adapts well to life in containers.

CULTIVARS: 'Pretty in Pink' has clear pink flowers with darker pink centers on 14-inch (35 cm) tall stems.

Celosia cristata   Amaranthaceae

CELOSIA

Plumed celosia has feathery flower spikes. Pinching off the stem tips in early summer will promote branching and more but smaller flower plumes.

OTHER COMMON NAMES: Cockscomb, plumed celosia.

DESCRIPTION: These tender perennials are grown as tender annuals. Their sturdy stems carry oval to narrow, pointed leaves that are green or tinted with bronze. The flowers can bloom all summer until frost in shades of fiery red, pink, orange, or yellow.

HEIGHT AND SPREAD: Height usually 12–24 inches (30–60 cm); spread to 12 inches (30 cm). Height and spread can vary widely, depending on the cultivar.

BEST SITE: Full sun; average, well-drained soil with added organic matter.

GROWING GUIDELINES: Celosias can be tricky to get started but are easy once established. If plants are disturbed during transplanting, later growth may be slow and stunted. For best results, sow seed directly into the garden after the last frost date, or buy small transplants. If you want to grow your own, sow seed indoors about 4 weeks before your last frost date. Plant seed ⅛ inch (3 mm) deep in individual pots. Set transplants out 12 weeks after the last frost date, when the soil is warm. Space compact types 6–8 inches (15–20 cm) apart; allow 1–2 feet (30–60 cm) between tall cultivars.

LANDSCAPE USES: Grow in groups or masses to show off the unusual flowers. Use compact types to edge beds and walkways and to accent container gardens and window boxes. Silver-leaved plants such as

CELOSIA—CONTINUED

CORNFLOWER

Cockscomb has tiny flowers clustered into dense, velvety, ruffled heads. Tall-stemmed types may need staking to keep the heavy heads from falling over.

Stick brushy prunings into the ground around young cornflower plants to support the stems as they grow. Pinching off spent blooms can prolong the flowering season.

dusty miller, lamb's-ears (*Stachys byzantina*), and snow-in-summer (*Cerastium tomentosum*) really show off celosia's glowing colors. Include some celosia in the cutting garden for fresh or dried arrangements.

To dry the flowers, harvest stems as soon as the flower heads reach the size you want; then hang them upside down in a dark, dry place.

CULTIVARS: 'Cristata Nana Mixed' has crested flowers in a range of colors on 1-foot (30 cm) tall stems. 'Red Velvet' has crested, purplish red flower heads to 10 inches (25 cm) across on stems up to 30 inches (75 cm) tall. 'Fairy Fountains Mixed' has 6-inch (15 cm) plumes in a range of colors on 15-inch (37.5 cm) tall stems. 'Century Mixed' has green or bronze leaves and 1-foot (30 cm) plumes in a mix of colors; plants grow 24–30 inches (60–75 cm) tall. 'New Look' grows to 10 inches (25 cm) tall and has deep red plumes over bronzy red leaves.

OTHER SPECIES:

C. spicata, wheat celosia, produces short, dense flower spikes on 2-4 foot (60-120 cm) stems. 'Flamingo Feather' has 4-8 inch (10-20 cm) spikes that are soft pink at the tips fading to pinkish white at the base.

OTHER COMMON NAMES: Bachelor's buttons.

DESCRIPTION: This is a dependable, easy-care, hardy annual. The bushy plants have narrow, lance-shaped, silvery green leaves and thin stems topped with fluffy flower heads. The 1–2-inch (2.5–5 cm) flowers bloom through the summer in white or shades of blue, purple, pink, or red.

HEIGHT AND SPREAD: Height 12–30 inches (30–75 cm); spread to 12 inches (30 cm).

BEST SITE: Full sun; average, well-drained soil.

GROWING GUIDELINES: Grows easily from seed sown directly into the garden in early fall (in mild-winter areas) or early spring. Plant seed ⅛ inch (3 mm) deep. To extend the flowering season from an early-spring planting, sow again every 2–4 weeks until midsummer. Other ways to establish cornflowers include buying transplants in spring or starting the seed indoors about 8 weeks before your last frost date. Set plants outdoors about 2 weeks before the last frost date. Space or thin plants to stand 8–12 inches (20–30 cm) apart. Cornflowers will self-sow if you leave a few flowers to set seed.

LANDSCAPE USES: Cornflowers are charming in meadow gardens and flower beds. They are also excellent for the cutting garden as fresh or dried flowers. Try compact cultivars in container gardens.

CULTIVARS: 'Jubilee Gem' has deep blue flowers on 1-foot (30 cm) stems.

| *Cheiranthus cheiri* | Cruciferae | *Chrysanthemum parthenium* | Compositae |

WALLFLOWER

FEVERFEW

The fragrant blooms of wallflowers are normally orange or yellow, but they also bloom in shades of red, pink, or creamy white. The flowers are ideal for spring arrangements.

DESCRIPTION: This perennial is commonly grown as a half-hardy annual or biennial for spring color. The bushy clumps of slender green leaves are topped with clusters of 1-inch (2.5 cm) wide four-petaled flowers from midspring to early summer.

HEIGHT AND SPREAD: Height 12–24 inches (30–60 cm); spread to 12 inches (30 cm).

BEST SITE: Full sun to partial shade; average to moist, well-drained soil, ideally with a neutral to slightly alkaline pH.

GROWING GUIDELINES: To grow as annuals, sow outdoors in early spring or indoors about 8 weeks before your last frost date. Plant seed ¼ inch (6 mm) deep. Set plants out 8–12 inches (20–30 cm) apart around the last frost date. In frost-free areas, grow wallflowers as biennials. Sow seed in pots or in a nursery bed in early summer; move plants to their flowering position in early fall. Water during dry spells to keep the soil evenly moist. Pull out plants when they have finished blooming.

LANDSCAPE USES: Grow in masses or in flower beds for spots of early color. One classic combination is orange wallflowers underplanted with blue forget-me-nots (*Myosotis sylvatica*). Wallflowers also combine beautifully with tulips.

CULTIVARS: 'Tom Thumb Mixed' blooms in a range of colors on 6–9-inch (15–22.5 cm) plants.

Feverfew is pretty but can become a pest by dropping lots of seed. Cutting off bloom stalks after the flowers fade will prevent this problem and promote new leafy growth.

DESCRIPTION: This short-lived perennial or biennial is often grown as a hardy annual. The plants form ferny mounds of deeply cut, aromatic, green leaves. The leafy stems are topped with 1-inch (2.5 cm) wide, single or double flowers, mainly in early- to mid-summer. The white or yellow, daisy-like flowers have yellow centers.

HEIGHT AND SPREAD: Height 12–30 inches (30–75 cm); spread 12–18 inches (30–45 cm).

BEST SITE: Full sun to partial shade; average, well-drained soil.

GROWING GUIDELINES: Starts easily from seed sown in the garden in mid- to late-spring. You can also start seed indoors 6–8 weeks before your last frost date. Plant the fine seed in a pot, press it lightly into the soil, and enclose the pot in a plastic bag until seedlings appear. Move young plants outdoors after the last frost date. Space plants or thin seedlings to stand 8–12 inches (20–30 cm) apart.

LANDSCAPE USES: Grow feverfew in flower beds and borders, herb gardens, and container gardens. It looks especially charming with roses in cottage gardens. The sprays of small flowers are great in fresh arrangements, too.

CULTIVARS: 'Golden Ball' grows to 12 inches (30 cm) tall, with golden yellow pompon-like flowers. 'Aureum' (also sold as *Pyrethrum aureum*) has single white flowers and ferny, bright yellow-green leaves.

Cleome hasslerana   Capparaceae   *Cobaea scandens*   Polemoniaceae

CLEOME

CUP-AND-SAUCER VINE

Cleome is a must for butterfly gardens; it's also popular with bees. Plant it in large groupings to show off the spidery white, pink, or rosy lavender flowers.

OTHER COMMON NAMES: Spider flower.

DESCRIPTION: Cleome is a fast-growing half-hardy annual. Its tall, sturdy stems and palm-like leaves are slightly sticky and have a musky (some say skunk-like) odor. Small spines form on the stems and on the undersides of the leaves. From midsummer until midfall, the stems are topped with globes of four-petaled flowers. Long stamens protrude from the flowers, giving them a spidery look. The blooms are followed by long, narrow seedpods.

HEIGHT AND SPREAD: Height 3–4 feet (90–120 cm); spread 18 inches (45 cm).

BEST SITE: Full sun to light shade; average, well-drained soil with added organic matter.

GROWING GUIDELINES: Easy to grow from seed sown directly in the garden in mid- to late-spring. For earlier bloom, buy transplants or start your own by sowing seed indoors about 4 weeks before your last frost date. Lightly press the seed into the surface, then enclose the pot in a plastic bag until seedlings appear. Set plants out around the last frost date. Space transplants or thin seedlings to stand 12 inches (30 cm) apart. Cleome usually self-sows prolifically. Pinching off seedpods regularly can reduce or eliminate self-sown seedlings.

LANDSCAPE USES: Try cleome in the back of flower beds and borders. Its delicate blooms look particularly nice in cottage gardens.

The bell-shaped flowers of cup-and-saucer vine open light green and age to purple or white; mature flowers have a sweet, honey-like fragrance.

OTHER COMMON NAMES: Cathedral bells, Mexican ivy.

DESCRIPTION: This vigorous, tender perennial climber is grown as a half-hardy annual. It has compound leaves, as well as tendrils that help the stems climb. From late summer until frost, inflated buds on long stalks open to 2-inch (5 cm) long, bell-shaped flowers. Short, green, petal-like bracts surround the base of each bell.

HEIGHT AND SPREAD: Vines can grow to 10 feet (3 m) or more; ultimate height and width depends on the size of its support.

BEST SITE: Full sun (or afternoon shade in hot-summer areas); average to moist, well-drained soil with added organic matter.

GROWING GUIDELINES: Before planting, make sure you have a sturdy support in place for the vines to climb on. Sow seed indoors 8–10 weeks before your last frost date. Soak the flat seeds in warm water overnight, then plant them on their edge in peat pots. Sow two or three seeds ¼ inch (6 mm) deep in each pot. Once seedlings emerge, clip off extras to leave one per pot. Set plants out 12 inches (30 cm) apart after the last frost date.

LANDSCAPE USES: This is a super screening plant for quick shade or privacy. It also makes a wonderful background plant for cottage gardens.

CULTIVARS: 'Alba' has green-tinted white flowers.

| *Coleus* x *hybridus* | Labiatae | *Consolida ambigua* | Ranunculaceae |

COLEUS

ROCKET LARKSPUR

Keep favorite coleus plants from year to year by taking cuttings in summer; they'll root quickly in water. Pot up the cuttings for winter; then put them outdoors in spring.

Tall cultivars of rocket larkspur may need support to stay upright. Push pieces of twiggy brush into the ground around young plants to hold them up as they grow.

DESCRIPTION: These tender perennials are grown as bushy, tender annuals. Their sturdy, square stems carry showy, patterned leaves with scalloped or ruffled edges. Each leaf can have several different colors, with zones, edges, or splashes in shades of red, pink, orange, yellow, and cream.

HEIGHT AND SPREAD: Height 6–24 inches (15–60 cm); spread 8–12 inches (20–30 cm).

BEST SITE: Partial shade; average to moist, well-drained soil with added organic matter.

GROWING GUIDELINES: Buy transplants in spring, or start your own by sowing seed indoors 8–10 weeks before your last frost date. Don't cover the seed; just press it lightly into the soil and enclose the pot in a plastic bag until seedlings appear. Set plants out 8–12 inches (20–30 cm) apart after the last frost. During the summer, water during dry spells. Pinch off the spikes of the pale blue flowers to promote more leafy growth.

LANDSCAPE USES: Coleus are great for adding all-season color to beds, borders, and container plantings. Groups of mixed leaf patterns can look too busy when combined with flowering plants, so grow them alone in masses, or consider sticking with a single leaf pattern.

CULTIVARS: 'Rainbow Mixed' has broad, scalloped leaves in a variety of colors on 20-inch (50 cm) tall plants.

OTHER COMMON NAMES: Larkspur.

DESCRIPTION: This hardy annual is grown for its showy flowers. The plants produce tall stems with finely divided, bright green leaves. Spikes of purple-blue, rose, pink, or white flowers bloom atop the stems from late spring through summer. There is a curving spur on the back of each flower. Rocket larkspur is also listed in seed catalogs as *C. ajacis*, *Delphinium ajacis*, and *D. consolida*.

HEIGHT AND SPREAD: Height to 1 foot (30 cm) for dwarf types, up to 4 feet (1.2 m) for tall cultivars; spread to 1 foot (30 cm).

BEST SITE: Full sun; average, well-drained soil with added organic matter.

GROWING GUIDELINES: Grows best from seed sown directly into the garden. Plant seed ¼ inch (6 mm) deep in fall or early spring. If you choose to start seedlings indoors, sow seed in individual peat pots 6–8 weeks before your last frost date. Set seedlings out in mid- to late-spring. Thin or space plants to stand 8–12 inches (20–30 cm) apart.

LANDSCAPE USES: Use the spiky flowers to add height and color to flower beds, borders, and cottage gardens. They mix well with perennials and also make great cut flowers.

CULTIVARS: 'Giant Imperial Mixed' has double blue, pink, or white flowers on well-branched, 4-foot (1.2 m) plants.

DWARF MORNING GLORY

This compact, easy-to-grow, hardy annual blooms from mid-summer through early fall. The cultivar 'Royal Ensign' has rich blue flowers with a white-and-yellow center.

DESCRIPTION: Plants form bushy, spreading mounds of oval to narrow green leaves topped with showy, trumpet-shaped blooms. The 1½-inch (37 mm) wide flowers are deep purple-blue on the outside, with a starry white center and a bright yellow throat.

HEIGHT AND SPREAD: Height to 12 inches (30 cm); spread 8–18 inches (20–45 cm).

BEST SITE: Full sun is best, although plants can take some shade; average, well-drained soil.

GROWING GUIDELINES: For earliest flowering, sow seed indoors 6 weeks before your last frost date. Soak seed overnight, then plant it ¼ inch (6 mm) deep in individual peat pots. Dwarf morning glory also grows easily from seed sown directly into the garden after the last frost date. Set transplants or thin seedlings to stand 8 inches (20 cm) apart. Stick short pieces of twiggy brush into the soil around the young plants to support the stems. Water during dry spells. Pinch off spent flowers to prolong the bloom season.

LANDSCAPE USES: Grow near the front of flower beds and borders or in container gardens. It looks especially charming cascading out of window boxes and hanging baskets.

CULTIVARS: 'Dwarf Rainbow Flash' has blue, purple, rose, or pink flowers on 6-inch (15 cm) plants. 'White Ensign' has white flowers with a yellow center.

CALLIOPSIS

Calliopsis grows easily from direct-sown seed and needs little fussing. Shearing the plants back by one-third in mid- to late-summer can prolong the bloom season.

DESCRIPTION: Calliopsis is a colorful, fast-growing, hardy annual. Its wiry stems carry narrow, green leaves and 1–2-inch (2.5–5 cm) wide, single or double, daisy-like flowers. The flowers are usually golden yellow with maroon centers but may also be all yellow or all orange. Plants can bloom from midsummer until frost.

HEIGHT AND SPREAD: Height 24–36 inches (30–90 cm), depending on the cultivar; spread to 12 inches (30 cm).

BEST SITE: Full sun; average, well-drained soil.

GROWING GUIDELINES: Grows quickly from seed sown directly into the garden in early- to mid-spring. You can also sow seed ⅛ inch (3 mm) deep indoors about 6 weeks before your last frost date. Set plants out around the last frost date. Space transplants or thin seedlings to stand about 8 inches (20 cm) apart. Push twiggy brush into the soil around young plants of tall-growing cultivars to support the stems as they grow.

LANDSCAPE USES: Depend on calliopsis for adding fast, easy-care color to beds and borders. It also looks wonderful in meadow gardens. Grow some in the cutting garden for fresh arrangements. Try the compact cultivars in containers.

| *Cosmos bipinnatus* | Compositae | *Cosmos sulphureus* | Compositae |

COSMOS

YELLOW COSMOS

Use fast-growing cosmos to fill spaces left by early-blooming annuals and perennials. Pinch off spent flowers to encourage more bloom; leave a few to self-sow.

Yellow cosmos is generally trouble-free through the season. Add it to the cutting garden; the colorful blooms lend a cheerful touch to fresh arrangements.

DESCRIPTION: These popular half-hardy annuals are grown for their colorful blooms. The bushy plants bear many finely cut, green leaves. In late summer and fall, the stems are topped with white, pink, or rosy red flowers. The single or semidouble, daisy-like blooms can grow up to 4 inches (10 cm) across.

HEIGHT AND SPREAD: Height 3–4 feet (90–120 cm); spread to 18 inches (45 cm).

BEST SITE: Full sun is best, although plants can take partial shade; average to moist, well-drained soil.

GROWING GUIDELINES: For earliest blooms, buy transplants in spring or start seed indoors 3–4 weeks before your last frost date. Plant seed ¼ inch (6 mm) deep. Set plants out 1-2 weeks after the last frost date. You can also sow seed directly into the garden around the last frost date. Space transplants or thin seedlings to stand 6-12 inches (15-30 cm) apart. Pinch off stem tips in early summer to promote branching and more flowers. Push sturdy pieces of twiggy brush into the soil around young plants to support the stems as they grow, or stake individual stems as needed. Or just let the plants sprawl; they'll send up more flowering stems.

LANDSCAPE USES: Cosmos adds height and color to flower beds, borders, and meadows. Grow a few in the cutting garden for arrangements.

CULTIVARS: 'Sensation Mixed' has single blooms on 3–4-foot (90–120 cm) stems.

OTHER COMMON NAMES: Klondike cosmos.

DESCRIPTION: Yellow cosmos is a half-hardy annual that forms bushy mounds of deeply lobed, dark green leaves. The thin stems carry showy, single or semidouble, daisy-like flowers from late summer until frost. The yellow, orange, or red blooms are 1–2 inches (2.5–5 cm) wide.

HEIGHT AND SPREAD: Height 24–36 inches (60–90 cm); spread to 18 inches (45 cm).

BEST SITE: Full sun; average, well-drained soil.

GROWING GUIDELINES: To get the earliest flowers, start seed indoors 4–6 weeks before your last frost date. Plant seed ¼ inch (6 mm) deep. Set plants out after the last frost date. Also grows easily from seed sown directly into the garden around the last frost date. Set plants or thin seedlings to about 12 inches (30 cm) apart. Pinching off spent flowers can prolong the bloom season. If you leave a few flowers to mature at the end of the season, plants will self-sow.

LANDSCAPE USES: Yellow cosmos is hard to beat for bright late-season color in flower beds, borders, and container gardens. The bushy plants also make great fillers in spaces left by spring-blooming annuals and perennials.

CULTIVARS: 'Bright Lights Mixed' has semidouble blooms in red, orange, or yellow on 3-foot (90 cm) tall stems. 'Sunny Red' has brilliant scarlet blooms on 12-inch (30 cm) tall plants.

| *Dianthus barbatus* | Caryophyllaceae | *Dianthus chinensis* | Caryophyllaceae |

SWEET WILLIAM

CHINA PINK

Sweet Williams may rebloom the following year if you shear them back after flowering, but you'll generally get a better show by starting new plants each year.

China pinks look equally lovely in beds, borders, and container plantings. Pinching off spent flowers can be time-consuming, but it will prolong the bloom season.

DESCRIPTION: This short-lived perennial is grown as a hardy biennial or annual. An old-fashioned favorite, it forms clumps of narrow, lance-shaped, green leaves. The stems are topped with dense, slightly rounded clusters of five-petaled flowers in early- to mid-summer. Each fragrant bloom is ¼–½ inch (6–12 mm) wide. Red, pink, and white are the most common colors; some flowers have eyes, or zones of contrasting colors.

HEIGHT AND SPREAD: Height 12–18 inches (30–45 cm); spread 8–12 inches (20–30 cm).

BEST SITE: Full sun to partial shade; average, well-drained soil.

GROWING GUIDELINES: For earliest bloom, grow as a biennial: Sow seed outdoors in pots or in a nursery bed in summer, then move plants to their garden position in fall. For bloom the same year, sow seed indoors (just barely cover it) about 8 weeks before your last frost date. Set plants out 2–3 weeks before the last frost date. Space transplants 8–10 inches (20–25 cm) apart. Sweet William will self-sow if you leave a few flowers to form seeds.

LANDSCAPE USES: Sweet William looks super as an early-summer filler for beds and borders. Its fragrant flowers are ideal for fresh arrangements.

CULTIVARS: 'Roundabout Mixed' has bicolored flowers in white, pink, rose, and red on compact, 6-inch (25 cm) tall plants.

OTHER COMMON NAMES: Rainbow pink.

DESCRIPTION: This biennial or short-lived perennial is usually grown as an annual. Plants form tufts of narrow, green leaves. The upright stems bear 1-inch (2.5 cm) wide, flat flowers with broad petals that are fringed at the tips. The white, pink, or red flowers bloom through the summer. China pinks have also been hybridized to produce more colorful and larger flowers over a longer season.

HEIGHT AND SPREAD: Height 8–12 inches (20–30 cm); similar spread.

BEST SITE: Full sun (afternoon shade in hot-summer areas); average, well-drained soil.

GROWING GUIDELINES: Buy plants in spring, or start seed indoors (just barely cover it) 6–8 weeks before your last frost date. You can also sow seed directly into the garden 2–3 weeks before the last frost date. Thin seedlings or set transplants to stand 6–8 inches (15–20 cm) apart.

LANDSCAPE USES: China pinks are a natural choice for cottage gardens. They also make colorful edgings for flower beds and walkways. Try a few in container gardens, too.

CULTIVARS: 'Telstar' blooms from summer into fall in a range of white, pinks, reds, and bicolors on 6–8-inch (15–20 cm) tall stems. 'Snowfire' grows to 8 inches (20 cm) tall and has white, fringed flowers with a red center.

Digitalis purpurea Scrophulariaceae

COMMON FOXGLOVE

Cut down the spent flower stems of common foxgloves after bloom to keep the garden tidy, or allow the seeds to form so plants can self-sow.

DESCRIPTION: This beautiful biennial or short-lived perennial is grown for its showy blooms. During the first year, plants form mounds of broad, velvety, grayish green leaves. In early- to mid-summer of the following year, the rosettes send up long, graceful spikes topped with thimble-shaped flowers. The 2–3-inch (57.5 cm) blooms may be white, cream, pink, or pinkish purple and often have contrasting spots on the inside.

HEIGHT AND SPREAD: Height 3–5 feet (90–150 cm); spread to 2 feet (60 cm).

BEST SITE: Full sun to partial shade (afternoon shade in hot-summer areas); average, well-drained soil with added organic matter.

GROWING GUIDELINES: Grow most foxgloves as biennials by sowing outdoors in pots or in a nursery bed in late summer. Sow the seed on the soil surface, press it in lightly, and keep the soil moist until seedlings appear. Move plants to their garden positions in fall. Space them about 12 inches (30 cm) apart. Tall cultivars may need staking.

LANDSCAPE USES: Grow them in the back of borders, where other plants will fill the space left in midsummer. The tall spires also look super in masses in lightly shaded woodlands.

CULTIVARS: 'Foxy Mixed' blooms the first year from seed (sow indoors 8–10 weeks before your last frost date) on 3–4-foot (90–120 cm) tall stems.

Dolichos lablab Leguminosae

HYACINTH BEAN

Once established, hyacinth bean is usually trouble-free. It makes an eye-catching garden accent when trained to grow up a trellis or climb a tripod of stakes in a border.

DESCRIPTION: This tender perennial climber is grown as a tender annual. The twining stems carry green or purplish leaves, each with three leaflets. The pinkish purple or white summer flowers are ¾ inch (18 cm) long; they bloom in spiky clusters. The lightly scented flowers are followed by glossy, deep purple seedpods. Hyacinth bean is also sold as *Lablab purpureus* and *Dipogon lablab*.

HEIGHT AND SPREAD: Height to 15 feet (4.5 m) or more; ultimate height and spread depend on the size of the support.

BEST SITE: Full sun; average, well-drained soil.

GROWING GUIDELINES: Before planting, install a support for the vine to climb. Hyacinth beans grow quickly from seed sown directly in the garden 2 weeks after the last frost date, when the soil is warm. Plant the seed ½ inch (12 mm) deep, with the white eye facing down. Soaking seed in water overnight before planting can help speed up germination. You can get an earlier start in cool-summer areas by sowing indoors 4–6 weeks before your last frost date. Plant two or three seeds in each pot, then thin seedlings to one per pot. Set plants out after the last frost date. Space transplants or thin seedlings to stand 8–12 inches (20–30 cm) apart.

LANDSCAPE USES: Use this fast-growing vine for quick shade or privacy or as a backdrop for a flower bed along a wall or arbor.

| *Eschscholzia californica* | Papaveraceae | *Euphorbia marginata* | Euphorbiaceae |

CALIFORNIA POPPY

SNOW-ON-THE-MOUNTAIN

The cup-shaped flowers of California poppy open during sunny days but close in cloudy weather and at night. Pinch off developing seedpods to prolong the bloom season.

Shrubby snow-on-the-mountain forms showy clumps of white-marked leaves by late summer. Use this old-fashioned favorite as a filler or accent plant in beds and borders.

DESCRIPTION: This tender perennial is usually grown as a hardy annual. Plants form loose clumps of deeply cut, blue-green leaves. The thin stems are topped with pointed buds that unfurl into single, semidouble, or double flowers up to 3 inches (7.5 cm) across in early summer through early fall. The silky-looking petals are usually orange or yellow, but they can also bloom in white, pink, or red.

HEIGHT AND SPREAD: Height 12–18 inches (30–45 cm); spread 6–12 inches (15–30 cm).

BEST SITE: Full sun; average to sandy, well-drained soil.

GROWING GUIDELINES: California poppy transplants poorly, so it's usually not worth starting seed indoors. Plants will grow quickly from seed sown directly into the garden in very early spring (or even in fall in frost-free areas). Scatter the seed over the soil surface and rake it in lightly. Thin seedlings to stand 6 inches (15 cm) apart. If blooms are sparse by midsummer, cut plants back by about one-third to encourage a new flush of flowers. Plants usually self-sow in mild-winter areas.

LANDSCAPE USES: California poppies are colorful, easy-to-grow fillers for flower beds and borders. They're also excellent in meadow gardens.

CULTIVARS: 'Thai Silk Mixed' grows to 10 inches (25 cm) tall and has semidouble flowers in shades of red, pink, orange, and gold. 'Dalli' has yellow-centered, scarlet flowers on 12-inch (30 cm) tall stems.

DESCRIPTION: This half-hardy annual is grown for its showy foliage. Young plants produce upright stems with oblong to pointed, green leaves. In mid- to late-summer, the stems begin to branch more, and the leaves produced on the upper parts of the branches are edged with white. At the branch tips, clusters of tiny flowers are surrounded by pure white, petal-like bracts.

HEIGHT AND SPREAD: Height 24–48 inches (60–120 cm); spread 12–18 inches (30–45 cm).

BEST SITE: Full sun; average, well-drained soil.

GROWING GUIDELINES: For earliest color, start seed ½ inch (12 mm) deep indoors 4–6 weeks before your last frost date. Set plants out after the last frost date. Or sow seed directly into the garden around the last frost date. Thin seedlings or space transplants to stand 12 inches (30 cm) apart. Plants may lean or flop by late summer; prevent this by staking plants in early- to mid-summer, while they're still young. Plants often self-sow.

LANDSCAPE USES: Use as a shrubby filler or accent in flower beds and borders. The showy leaves are especially nice in arrangements, so include a few plants in the cutting garden. Handle cut stems carefully, though; they will leak a milky sap that can irritate your skin, eyes, and mouth.

CULTIVARS: 'Summer Icicle' grows to a compact 18 inches (45 cm) tall.

| *Eustoma grandiflorum* | Gentianaceae | *Gaillardia pulchella* | Compositae |

PRAIRIE GENTIAN

Prairie gentian looks lovely planted in masses with shrubs or alone in a container. The gorgeous blooms can last several weeks in fresh arrangements.

DESCRIPTION: This beautiful but slow-growing biennial is generally grown as a half-hardy annual. Its slender, upright stems carry oblong, gray-green leaves and are topped with pointed buds. The buds unfurl to produce long-lasting, single or double flowers that resemble poppies or roses. The 2–3-inch (57.5 cm) flowers bloom in white and shades of cream, pink, rose, and purple-blue.

HEIGHT AND SPREAD: Height usually 12–24 inches; spread to 12 inches (30 cm).

BEST SITE: Full sun to partial shade; average, well-drained soil.

GROWING GUIDELINES: You'll get the quickest results by buying transplants in spring. If you want to try raising your own, sow them indoors in January. Scatter the seed over the pot surface, press it lightly into the soil, and enclose the pot in a plastic bag until seedlings appear. Set transplants out 1-2 weeks after your last frost date. Space them about 6 inches (15 cm) apart in clumps of three or more plants. Pinching off stems tips once or twice in early summer will promote branching and more blooms. Remove spent blooms to prolong flowering.

LANDSCAPE USES: Prairie gentian is an elegant addition to any flower bed or border.

CULTIVARS: 'Double Eagle Mixed' has double flowers in a range of colors and bicolors on 24-inch (60 cm) tall stems.

BLANKET FLOWER

Blanket flower blooms are often orange-red with yellow tips, but they may also be red, yellow, or orange around a reddish purple center.

DESCRIPTION: Blanket flower is a fast-growing hardy annual. Plants produce clumps of narrow, hairy, gray-green leaves highlighted all summer by bright flowers. The single or double, daisy-like blooms may be up to 3 inches (7.5 cm) wide, with toothed petals that give them a fringed appearance.

HEIGHT AND SPREAD: Height 12–24 inches (30–60 cm); similar spread.

BEST SITE: Full sun; average, well-drained to dry soil. Blanket flowers are heat- and drought-tolerant.

GROWING GUIDELINES: In most areas, you'll get best results by sowing seed directly into the garden. Plant seed ⅛ inch (3 mm) deep in spring around your last frost date (or even in fall in mild-winter areas). If your summers are short and cool, get an early start by sowing seed indoors 4–6 weeks before the last frost date. Space transplants or thin seedlings to stand 12 inches (30 cm) apart. Stick short pieces of twiggy brush into the ground around young plants to support the stems. Pinch off spent flowers to prolong the bloom season. Plants will self-sow if you allow a few flowers to set seed.

LANDSCAPE USES: Blanket flowers add loads of summer color to flower beds and borders. Grow a few in the cutting garden for fresh flowers.

CULTIVARS: 'Gaiety Mixed' grows to 24 inches (60 cm) tall and has double flowers in reds, oranges, yellows, and bicolors.

| *Helichrysum bracteatum* | Compositae | *Heliotropium arborescens* | Boraginaceae |

STRAWFLOWER

Cutting strawflowers for fresh arrangements or drying will promote branching and prolong the bloom season. The flowers dry quickly when hung upside down in a dark, airy place.

DESCRIPTION: This half-hardy annual is grown for its colorful, long-lasting blooms. The bushy plants have long, narrow, green leaves and daisy-like flower heads with stiff, papery, petal-like bracts. The flower heads bloom from midsummer until frost in white, pink, rose, red, orange, or yellow. Fully open flower heads are 1–2 inches (2.5–5 cm) wide and have yellow centers.

HEIGHT AND SPREAD: Height usually 24–48 inches (60–120 cm); spread to 12 inches (30 cm).

BEST SITE: Full sun; average, well-drained soil.

GROWING GUIDELINES: For earliest blooms, buy transplants or start your own by sowing seed indoors 6–8 weeks before your last frost date. Just press the seed lightly into the surface and enclose the pot in a plastic bag until seedlings appear. Set plants out 2 weeks after the last frost date. Or sow seed directly into the garden after the last frost date. Set transplants or thin seedlings to stand 10–12 inches (25–30 cm) apart.

LANDSCAPE USES: Strawflowers add lots of long-lasting color to flower beds and borders. Grow an ample supply in the cutting garden for drying, as well. Harvest flowers when they are about one-quarter open; they'll open more as they dry. The dried stems tend to be brittle, so it's best to remove them after harvest and insert a piece of floral wire into the base of the flower head.

COMMON HELIOTROPE

The violet, purple-blue, or white flowers of common heliotrope may have a vanilla- or cherry-like scent. Sniff the flowers before you buy to find the most fragrant ones.

OTHER COMMON NAMES: Cherry pie.

DESCRIPTION: This tender perennial is usually grown as a tender annual. Plants produce shrubby clumps of sturdy stems and hairy, deep to medium green, heavily veined, oval leaves. Clusters of ¼-inch (6 mm) wide, tubular flowers bloom atop the stems from summer until frost.

HEIGHT AND SPREAD: Height usually 24–36 inches (60–90 cm); spread 12–24 inches (30–60 cm).

BEST SITE: Full sun (to afternoon shade in hot-summer climates); average, well-drained soil with added organic matter.

GROWING GUIDELINES: Easiest to start from nursery-grown or overwintered plants. If you want to grow your own, sow seed indoors 10-12 weeks before your last frost date. Seed may take several weeks to germinate. Set plants out about 12 inches (30 cm) apart, 2–3 weeks after the last frost date. Pinch off the stem tips in early summer to promote branching and more flowers. Remove spent flower clusters. To overwinter plants, cut them back, then dig and pot them up before the first fall frost; or take stem cuttings in late summer.

LANDSCAPE USES: Grow in flower beds and borders or containers.

CULTIVARS: 'Marine' has deep purple, dense, rounded flower heads and purplish green leaves; fragrance is variable.

ANNUAL CANDYTUFT

GARDEN BALSAM

Annual candytuft needs little care and tends to self-sow. In hot-summer areas, pull out plants after bloom and replace them with summer- to fall-blooming annuals.

OTHER COMMON NAMES: Globe candytuft.

DESCRIPTION: This dependable, hardy annual forms mounds of narrow, green leaves on many-branched stems. The mounds are covered with dense, slightly rounded flower clusters approximately 2 inches (5 cm) across from late spring through midsummer. Each cluster contains many ¼–½ inch (6–12 mm) wide, four-petaled blooms. Flowers may be white, pink, pinkish purple, rose, or red.

HEIGHT AND SPREAD: Height 8–12 inches (20–30 cm); spread 8–10 inches (20–25 cm).

BEST SITE: Full sun to partial shade; average, well-drained soil.

GROWING GUIDELINES: For the earliest flowers, sow seed indoors 6–8 weeks before your last frost date. Plant seed ¼ inch (6 mm) deep. Set plants out around the last frost date. Annual candytuft also grows easily from seed sown directly into the garden. Make the first sowing in early- to mid-spring. Sowing again every 3–4 weeks until early summer can extend the bloom season until fall if your summer temperatures don't get much above 90°F (32°C). Thin seedlings or space plants to stand 6–8 inches (15–20 cm) apart.

LANDSCAPE USES: Annual candytuft makes a colorful edging or filler for flower beds and borders.

CULTIVARS: 'Dwarf Fairyland Mixed' grows to 8 inches (20 cm) tall with white, pink, or purplish blooms.

The bright flowers of garden balsam bloom near the tops of the stems, among the lance-shaped, green leaves. This old-fashioned favorite can grow in sun if the soil is moist.

DESCRIPTION: This tender annual has a bushy, upright habit. The 1–2-inch (2.5–5 cm) wide, single or double flowers bloom from midsummer until frost, usually in white or shades of pink, purple-pink, rose, or red.

HEIGHT AND SPREAD: Height 24–30 inches (60–75 cm); spread to 18 inches.

BEST SITE: Full sun to partial shade; average to moist, well-drained soil with added organic matter.

GROWING GUIDELINES: Garden balsam is sometimes sold as transplants, but it is also easy to start from seed. To grow your own transplants, sow seed indoors 6–8 weeks before your last frost date. Press the seed lightly into the soil surface and enclose the pot in a plastic bag until seedlings appear. Set plants out 1-2 weeks after the last frost date. You can also sow seed directly into the garden after the last frost date. Plant seed ⅛ inch (3 mm) deep and keep the soil moist until seedlings appear. Thin seedlings or space transplants 12-16 inches (30-40 cm) apart. Water during dry spells. Plants often self-sow freely.

LANDSCAPE USES: The lovely flowers and foliage of garden balsam add height and color to shady beds and borders. For the best show, set out three or more plants in each area to form lush clumps.

CULTIVARS: 'Camellia Flowered Mixed' has large, double flowers on 24-inch (60 cm) tall stems.

NEW GUINEA IMPATIENS

If you want a particular flower or leaf color, buy New Guinea impatiens as plants in spring. You can also start some types from seed.

DESCRIPTION: These tender perennials are usually grown as tender annuals. The bushy, well-branched plants have large, pointed, green or reddish bronze leaves; the leaves are sometimes striped with pink, red, or yellow. Vibrant pink, red, orange, purple, or white flowers to 3 inches (7.5 cm) across bloom atop the plants from June until frost.

HEIGHT AND SPREAD: Height 12–24 inches (30–60 cm); spread 12–18 inches (20–45 cm).

BEST SITE: Full sun to partial shade; average to moist, well-drained soil with added organic matter.

GROWING GUIDELINES: Most New Guinea impatiens are grown from cuttings, so you can buy plants with the colors you like best in spring. Some are available from seed; sow indoors (just barely cover with soil) 6–8 weeks before your last frost date. Set plants out 12-18 inches apart 1-2 weeks after your last frost date. Plants are sometimes difficult to over-winter indoors, but if you want to keep a particular plant, try taking stem cuttings in summer. Pot up rooted cuttings and keep them in a sunny window until the following spring.

LANDSCAPE USES: Enjoy the showy leaves and jewel-like flowers in beds, borders, and containers.

CULTIVARS: 'Spectra Hybrid Mixed' grows 12–18 inches (30–45 cm) tall and has green, bronze, or variegated leaves and white, pink, red, peach, orange, lavender, or purplish flowers.

IMPATIENS

A mixed planting of impatiens makes a colorful annual groundcover under trees and shrubs. For good growth, they need moist soil; mulch them and water during dry spells.

OTHER COMMON NAMES: Busy Lizzie, patient Lucy, patience, sultana.

DESCRIPTION: Impatiens are tender perennials usually grown as tender annuals. Plants form neat, shrubby mounds of well-branched, succulent stems; the lance-shaped, green or bronze-brown leaves have slightly scalloped edges. The plants are covered with flat, spurred flowers up to 2 inches (5 cm) wide from late spring until frost. The single or double blooms may be white, pink, red, orange, or lavender; some have an eye, or swirls of contrasting colors. The flowers are followed by swollen, ribbed seedpods that burst open when ripe, flinging seeds far and wide.

HEIGHT AND SPREAD: Height 6–24 inches (15–60 cm), depending on the cultivar; similar spread.

BEST SITE: Partial to full shade; average to moist, well-drained soil with added organic matter.

GROWING GUIDELINES: Transplants of these popular annuals are usually available for sale in spring in a variety of plant heights and flower colors. You can also start your own by sowing seed indoors 8–10 weeks before your last frost date. Don't cover the seed; just press it lightly into the soil surface. Enclose the pot in a plastic bag and keep it in a warm place until seedlings appear. Young seedlings tend to grow slowly. Set transplants out about 2 weeks after your last frost date. Space

MOONFLOWER

Light-colored impatiens tend to really stand out in shady spots. Their soft shades also blend beautifully with many other shade-lovers, such as ferns and hostas.

Before planting moonflowers, set up some kind of support, such as vertical wires or a trellis. Other than watering during dry spells, the plants need little care.

compact types 6–8 inches (15–20 cm) apart and tall cultivars 12–18 inches (30–45 cm) apart.

Mulch plants to keep their roots moist and water during dry spells. Other than that, these low-maintenance plants don't need much care to keep blooming through the season. Summer stem cuttings root quickly in water. Plant rooted cuttings in the garden in mid- to late-summer to fill in any gaps, or pot them up for use as winter houseplants.

LANDSCAPE USES: Impatiens are the stars of shady gardens. Mix them with other annuals and perennials in beds and borders, or grow them alone in masses under trees and large shrubs. Impatiens also perform well in pots, window boxes, and hanging baskets with regular watering.

CULTIVARS: 'Super Elfin Hybrid Mixed' blooms in a range of colors on 8–10-inch (20–25 cm) tall, well-branched plants; 'Super Elfin Swirl' has soft pink flowers that have deep rose pink edges. 'Sparkles Mixed' has colorful flowers and bronzy green leaves on 12-inch (30 cm) tall plants. The flowers of 'Wink 'n' Blink Hybrid Mixed' have a showy eye of a contrasting color on 10-inch (25 cm) tall stems. 'Rosette Hybrid Mixed' grows to 18 inches (45 cm) tall and has single, semidouble, or double flowers in a range of colors.

DESCRIPTION: This tender perennial vine is usually grown as a tender annual. The twining stems produce heart-shaped leaves and pointed buds that unfurl into funnel-shaped to flat, white blooms up to 6 inches (15 cm) across. The fragrant summer flowers open in the evening and may stay open through the next morning. Moonflower is also listed in seed catalogs as *Calonyction aculeatum*.

HEIGHT AND SPREAD: Height to 10 feet (3 m) or more; ultimate height and spread depend on the size of the support the vine is climbing on.

BEST SITE: Full sun; average, well-drained soil.

GROWING GUIDELINES: For earliest flowers, start seed indoors 4–6 weeks before your last frost date. Soak seed in warm water overnight, then plant it 1 inch (2.5 cm) deep in peat pots (two or three seeds per pot). When seedlings appear, keep the strongest one in each pot and cut off the others in the same pot at the soil surface. Set plants out 1-2 weeks after the last frost date. If you have a long, warm growing season, you could instead sow seed directly into the garden after the last frost date, when the soil is warm. Set plants or thin seedlings to stand 12 inches (30 cm) apart.

LANDSCAPE USES: Use as a fast-growing screen for shade or privacy. Its night-blooming habit makes it an excellent choice for planting around decks and patios where you sit on summer evenings.

| *Ipomoea tricolor* | Convolvulaceae | *Kochia scoparia* f. *trichophylla* | Chenopodiaceae |

MORNING GLORY

SUMMER CYPRESS

Morning glories grow slowly at first, then really take off when the weather heats up in midsummer. Established vines are generally problem-free; they often self-sow freely.

Cut summer cypress plants to the ground in fall before the seed matures to keep plants from self-sowing; otherwise, you may have hundreds of seedlings next year!

DESCRIPTION: A tender perennial vine grown as a tender annual. This fast-growing climber has twining stems and heart-shaped, green leaves. The pointed buds open in early morning to reveal showy, trumpet-shaped flowers up to 5 inches (12.5 cm) across. Each flower lasts only 1 day, but new buds open every day through the summer.

HEIGHT AND SPREAD: Height to 8 feet (2.4 m) or more; ultimate height and spread depend on the size of the support morning glory is climbing on.

BEST SITE: Full sun; average, well-drained soil.

GROWING GUIDELINES: Before planting, make sure you have a sturdy trellis or some other support for the vines to climb. For earliest flowers, sow seed indoors 4 weeks before your last frost date. Soak seed in warm water overnight, then sow it ½ inch (12 mm) deep in peat pots. Plant two or three seeds in each pot, then thin to one seedling per pot. Set plants out 2 weeks after the last frost date. You can also start morning glories from seed sown directly into the garden after the last frost. Set plants or thin seedlings to stand 8–12 inches (20–30 cm) apart.

LANDSCAPE USES: Morning glory makes a good quick-growing screen for shade or privacy. It also looks great climbing through large shrubs or roses or on a trellis or wall behind a cottage garden.

CULTIVARS: 'Heavenly Blue' is a popular, free-blooming cultivar with sky blue, white-centered flowers.

OTHER COMMON NAMES: Burning bush, fire bush.

DESCRIPTION: This half-hardy annual is grown for its compact, shrubby clumps of foliage and attractive fall color. Plants form feathery, oval or rounded mounds of narrow, spring green leaves that take on purplish red tints when cool weather arrives. Tiny flowers bloom along the stems in early fall.

HEIGHT AND SPREAD: Height usually 3–4 feet (90–120 cm); spread to 2 feet (60 cm).

BEST SITE: Full sun; average, well-drained soil.

GROWING GUIDELINES: Get an early start on the season by sowing seed indoors 4–6 weeks before your last frost date. Don't cover the seed; just press it lightly into the soil surface and enclose the pot in a plastic bag until seedlings appear. Set plants out after the last frost date. You can also sow seed directly into the garden after the last frost date. Set transplants or thin seedlings to stand 24 inches apart (60 cm). (If you're growing summer cypress as a hedge, space plants 10–12 inches [25–30 cm] apart.) Plants will look spindly at first but fill in quickly. In windy or exposed areas, push pieces of twiggy brush into the soil around young plants to support the stems as they grow.

LANDSCAPE USES: Group several plants as a filler for the back of beds or borders, or use single plants as shrubby accents. Summer cypress also looks great as a temporary hedge.

| *Lathyrus odoratus* | Leguminosae | *Limonium sinuatum* | Plumbaginaceae |

SWEET PEA

ANNUAL STATICE

Dozens of sweet pea cultivars are available in a range of heights and colors. Many modern cultivars aren't very fragrant; check catalog descriptions to find scented types.

Annual statice is a natural for fresh or dried arrangements. To dry it, pick stems when the clusters are about three-quarters open; hang them in a dark, airy place.

DESCRIPTION: These old-fashioned hardy annuals are grown for their charming flowers. Plants produce leafy vines that climb by tendrils. Dainty, pea-like flowers to 2 inches (5 cm) long bloom on long, slender flower stems from midspring into summer. Flower colors are usually white or bright or pastel shades of pink, red, or purple. The flowers often have crimped or ruffled petals.

HEIGHT AND SPREAD: Height usually 4–6 feet (1.2–1.8 m); spread 6–12 inches (15–30 cm).

BEST SITE: Full sun (or afternoon shade in hot-summer areas); loose, evenly moist soil enriched with ample amounts of organic matter.

GROWING GUIDELINES: Before planting, set up some sort of string or netting trellis for the vines to climb. Start seed indoors 6–8 weeks before your last frost date. Soak seed in warm water overnight, then plant ½ inch (12 mm) deep in peat pots. Set plants out in midspring, after danger of heavy frost. Or sow seed directly into the garden in early spring. Set transplants or thin seedlings to stand 4–6 inches (10–15 cm) apart. Mulch plants to keep the roots cool and moist. Water during dry spells. Pull out the vines when they stop blooming in summer.

LANDSCAPE USES: Train sweet peas to climb a tripod of stakes as an early-season accent for beds, borders, and cottage gardens. Include them in the cutting garden for fresh cut flowers.

DESCRIPTION: This biennial or tender perennial is usually grown as a half-hardy annual. Plants form low rosettes of wavy-edged, green leaves that send up sturdy, winged stems in summer. The loosely branched stems are topped with flattened clusters of ¼-inch (6 mm) wide, white flowers, each surrounded by a papery, tubular calyx—the colorful part of the flower head. Annual statice comes in a rainbow of colors, including white, pink, peach, red, orange, yellow, purple, and blue.

HEIGHT AND SPREAD: Height 12–24 inches (30–60 cm); spread to 12 inches (30 cm).

BEST SITE: Full sun; average, well-drained soil.

GROWING GUIDELINES: Buy transplants in spring, or start your own by sowing seed indoors 6–8 weeks before your last frost date. Plant the seed ¼ inch (3 mm) deep. Move seedlings to individual pots when they have two or three sets of leaves. Plant them in the garden around the last frost date, or sow seed directly into the garden after the last frost date. Space transplants or thin seedlings to stand 8–10 inches (20–25 cm) apart. Established plants need little care.

LANDSCAPE USES: Annual statice is an unusual and attractive filler for flower beds and borders. Try the compact types in container gardens.

CULTIVARS: 'Petite Bouquet' has flowers in a range of colors on 12-inch (30 cm) stems.

| *Lobelia erinus* | Campanulaceae | *Lobularia maritima* | Cruciferae |

EDGING LOBELIA

If you grow edging lobelia from seed or buy seedlings in trays, transplant them in clumps (rather than separating them into individual plants) to avoid damaging the stems.

DESCRIPTION: This tender perennial is usually grown as a half-hardy annual. Plants form trailing or mounding clumps of slender stems with small, narrow, green leaves. Plants are covered with ½–¼-inch (12–18 mm) wide flowers from late spring until frost. The five-petaled flowers bloom in white and shades of blue, purple, and pinkish red.

HEIGHT AND SPREAD: Height 6–8 inches (15–20 cm); spread 6–10 inches (15–25 cm).

BEST SITE: Full sun to partial shade (especially in hot-summer areas); average, well-drained soil with added organic matter.

GROWING GUIDELINES: Buy transplants in spring, or start your own by sowing seed indoors 8–10 weeks before your last frost date. Don't cover the seed; just press it lightly into the soil and enclose the pot in a plastic bag until seedlings appear. Set plants out 6–8 inches (15–20 cm) apart after the last frost date. Water during dry spells. Shear plants back by half after each flush of bloom and fertilize to promote rebloom.

LANDSCAPE USES: Looks great along the front of beds and borders or as a filler among taller plants. Cascading types make attractive fillers for container gardens, window boxes, and hanging baskets until bushier plants fill in.

CULTIVARS: 'Crystal Palace' has dark green to bronze leaves and deep blue flowers on 6-inch (15 cm) plants.

SWEET ALYSSUM

Sweet alyssum may stop blooming during summer heat but will start again when cool weather returns. Shear off spent flowers and water thoroughly to promote new growth.

DESCRIPTION: Sweet alyssum is a tender perennial grown as a hardy annual. Plants form low mounds of many-branched stems and narrow, green leaves. Domed clusters of many ¼-inch (6 mm) blooms cover plants in summer and fall. The sweetly scented, four-petaled flowers bloom in white and shades of pink and purple. Sweet alyssum is also listed in seed catalogs as *Alyssum maritimum*.

HEIGHT AND SPREAD: Height 4–8 inches (10–20 cm); spread 10–12 inches (25–30 cm).

BEST SITE: Full sun to partial shade (especially in hot-summer areas); average, well-drained soil.

GROWING GUIDELINES: Buy transplants in spring, or start your own by sowing seed indoors 6–8 weeks before your last frost date. Just barely cover the seed with soil. Set plants out around the last frost date. Sweet alyssum also grows easily from seed sown directly into the garden in mid- to late-spring. Space transplants or thin seedlings to stand 6 inches (15 cm) apart. Plants usually self-sow.

LANDSCAPE USES: Grow as an edging or filler in flower beds and borders or as a groundcover under roses and shrubs. It also grows well in container gardens and window boxes.

CULTIVARS: 'Carpet of Snow' has pure white flowers on spreading plants to 4 inches (10 cm) tall. 'Royal Carpet' is similar but has bright purple flowers.

HONESTY   VIRGINIA STOCK

Honesty is a hardy biennial grown for its pretty flowers and showy dried seedpods. Leave a few plants in the garden to self-sow; harvest the rest for arrangements.

OTHER COMMON NAMES: Money plant, silver dollar.

DESCRIPTION: First-year plants form clumps of coarse, heart-shaped, hairy, green leaves. In the second spring, the clumps send up loosely branched stems topped with elongated clusters of ½-inch (12 mm) wide, four-petaled flowers. The lightly fragrant, purple-pink blooms are followed by flat, circular seedpods with papery outer skins and a satiny white central disk.

HEIGHT AND SPREAD: Height 18–36 inches (45–90 cm) in bloom; spread to 12 inches (30 cm).

BEST SITE: Partial shade; average, well-drained soil (added organic matter is a plus).

GROWING GUIDELINES: Buy and set out nursery-grown plants in early spring for bloom the same year, or start your own from seed for bloom next year. Sow seed directly into the garden, ⅛–¼ inch (3–6 mm) deep, in spring or late summer. Set transplants or thin seedlings to stand about 12 inches (30 cm) apart.

LANDSCAPE USES: The flowers add color to spring beds and borders. The white-flowered forms look especially nice in woodland gardens. Honesty is also a traditional favorite in cutting gardens for its dried seedpods. When the seedpods turn beige, cut the stems off at ground level and bring them indoors. Once seedpods feel dry, gently peel off the outer skins to reveal the silvery center membrane.

Virginia stock can bloom in as little as 4 weeks from seed sown directly into the garden. Sow every 3 to 4 weeks through midsummer to have flowers from summer until frost.

DESCRIPTION: The upright, branching stems of this fast-growing hardy annual carry small, pointed, grayish green leaves. Flat, four-petaled, lightly fragrant flowers bloom in loose clusters atop the stems. The purple, pink, or white flowers are ¼–½ inch (6–12 mm) wide.

HEIGHT AND SPREAD: Height 6–8 inches (15–20 cm); spread to 4 inches (10 cm).

BEST SITE: Full sun to partial shade (in hot-summer areas); average, well-drained soil.

GROWING GUIDELINES: Grows best from seed sown directly in the garden. For the longest bloom season, sow at 3–4 week intervals from early spring through midsummer. (In mild-winter areas, you can sow in fall for even earlier spring bloom.) Rake the seedbed to cover the seed lightly, then keep the soil moist until seedlings appear. Thin seedlings to stand 3–4 inches (7.5–10 cm) apart. Plants may self-sow freely.

LANDSCAPE USES: Virginia stock makes a nice filler or edging annual for flower beds and borders. The flowers are very popular with bees.

| *Matthiola incana* | Cruciferae | *Mimulus* x *hybridus* | Scrophulariaceae |

COMMON STOCK

MONKEY FLOWER

The fragrant, single or double flowers of common stock bloom in white and shades of pink, red, yellow, and purple. They are wonderful in the garden or in arrangements.

You can overwinter monkey flowers indoors by digging and potting up plants before frost or by rooting stem cuttings in late summer; grow them in a cool, sunny room.

DESCRIPTION: This biennial or short-lived perennial is usually grown as a hardy annual. The fast-growing, bushy plants have upright stems and lance-shaped, grayish leaves. The stems are topped with spikes of four-petaled, 1-inch (2.5 cm) wide flowers in summer.

HEIGHT AND SPREAD: Height 12–24 inches (30–60 cm); spread to 12 inches (30 cm).

BEST SITE: Full sun; average, well-drained soil with added organic matter.

GROWING GUIDELINES: Grows easily from seed sown directly into the garden. Make the first sowing about 1 month before your last frost date. To extend the bloom season, make another sowing in late spring or early summer. (In mild-winter areas, you can also sow in late summer for winter and early-spring bloom.) Scatter seed on the soil surface, then rake lightly to just cover the seed. Keep the seedbed moist until seedlings appear. Thin seedlings to stand 6–8 inches apart. Mulch plants to keep the roots cool and moist. Water during dry spells.

LANDSCAPE USES: Use as a filler in beds and borders near your house or outdoor sitting areas, where you can enjoy the fragrance.

OTHER SPECIES:

M. *longipetala* subsp. *bicornis*, evening-scented stock, has pale purple to white, night-blooming flowers on 12-inch (30 cm) tall stems.

DESCRIPTION: This tender perennial is grown as a half-hardy annual. Plants form clumps of green to reddish stems with oval, light green leaves that have toothed edges. Velvety, tubular flowers with flat faces bloom atop the plants through summer. The 2-inch (5 cm) flowers are usually yellow, orange, or red and are often dotted or splashed with other colors in the center.

HEIGHT AND SPREAD: Height 6–12 inches (15–30 cm); similar spread.

BEST SITE: Partial shade; moist soil. Plants can take full sun if they have evenly moist soil.

GROWING GUIDELINES: Start seed indoors 8–10 weeks before your last frost date. Scatter the dust-like seed over the soil surface, but don't cover it. Just press the seed lightly into the soil and enclose the pot in a plastic bag until seedlings appear. Set transplants out 6 inches (15 cm) apart after the last frost date. Water during dry spells. If plants stop blooming in hot weather, cutting them back halfway and watering thoroughly may promote rebloom.

LANDSCAPE USES: Monkey flowers add glowing color to moist-soil beds and borders. Try them as a groundcover in wet spots to fill in after spring-blooming primroses. They also look great in containers, but they'll need frequent watering.

CULTIVARS: 'Calypso' grows to 8 inches (20 cm) tall and has large flowers in yellow, orange, or red.

| *Mirabilis jalapa* Nyctaginaceae | *Myosotis sylvatica* Boraginaceae |

FOUR-O'CLOCK

FORGET-ME-NOT

Four-o'clocks have fragrant flowers that open in late after-noon. They tend to close the next morning, unless the weather is cloudy. Grow them in the garden or in pots.

Forget-me-not blooms are often sky blue with white or yellow centers, but they can also be pink or white. They are ideal companions for spring bulbs and other early annuals.

OTHER COMMON NAMES: Marvel-of-Peru.

DESCRIPTION: These tender perennials are usually grown as half-hardy annuals. The bushy, fast-growing plants have branching stems and oval to lance-shaped, deep green leaves. Trumpet-shaped, 1-inch (2.5 cm) wide flowers bloom from midsummer until frost in white or shades of pink, magenta, red, and yellow; sometimes different colors appear on the same plant.

HEIGHT AND SPREAD: Height usually 24–36 inches (60–90 cm); spread to 24 inches (60 cm).

BEST SITE: Full sun to partial shade; average, well-drained soil.

GROWING GUIDELINES: Four-o'clocks are gratify-ingly easy to grow from seed. For earliest bloom, start them indoors 4–6 weeks before your last frost date. Soak the seed in warm water overnight, then plant it ¼–½ inch (6–12 mm) deep in peat pots. Transplant seedlings to the garden about 2 weeks after the last frost date, when the soil is warm. You can also sow seed directly into the garden after the last frost date. Space transplants or thin seedlings to stand 12–18 inches (30–45 cm) apart. Plants may self-sow in mild areas.

LANDSCAPE USES: Plant clumps in the middle of flower beds and borders for a colorful filler. Grow a few around an outdoor sitting area, where you can enjoy the flowers and fragrance after a long day.

DESCRIPTION: These short-lived perennials are usu-ally grown as hardy biennials or annuals. Plants form dense clumps of narrow, lance-shaped, hairy leaves. Sprays of many ⅓-inch (8 mm) wide flowers bloom over the leaves from midspring through early summer.

HEIGHT AND SPREAD: Height usually 12–18 inches (30–45 cm); spread 8–10 inches (20–25 cm).

BEST SITE: Partial shade; average to moist, well-drained soil with added organic matter.

GROWING GUIDELINES: To grow forget-me-nots as biennials, sow seed outdoors in pots or in a nursery bed in spring or summer. Plant seed ⅛ inch (3 mm) deep. Move plants to the garden in early fall. For bloom the same year, buy plants in early spring, or start seed indoors 4–6 weeks before your last frost date. Set plants out 1-2 weeks before the last frost date. Space plants or thin seedlings to stand 6 inch-es (15 cm) apart. Water during dry spells. Shearing off spent flowers often promotes rebloom. Plants often self-sow freely.

LANDSCAPE USES: Forget-me-nots are invaluable for spring color in shady gardens. Try them as an early-season groundcover under shrubs, or grow them in beds and borders with short tulips and other spring bulbs for stunning color combinations.

CULTIVARS: 'Blue Ball' has blue flowers on compact, 6-inch (15 cm) tall plants.

ICELAND POPPY   CORN POPPY

Removing spent flower stems can prolong Iceland poppy's bloom season. As summer approaches and new growth slows, leave a few flowers to mature so plants can self-sow.

DESCRIPTION: This short-lived perennial is usually grown as a hardy biennial or annual. Plants form compact rosettes of hairy, deeply cut, gray-green leaves. Long, slender, leafless stems are topped with plump, hairy, nodding buds that open to bowl-shaped, four-petaled flowers. The 2–4-inch (2.5–5 cm) wide, lightly fragrant flowers have crinkled petals. They bloom mainly in early- to mid-summer in a range of vibrant colors, including white, pink, red, orange, and yellow.

HEIGHT AND SPREAD: Height 12–18 inches (30–45 cm); spread 4–6 inches (10–15 cm).

BEST SITE: Full sun; average, well-drained to dry soil. Grows poorly in hot weather.

GROWING GUIDELINES: Easiest to grow from seed sown directly into the garden. Plant in late fall or very early spring for summer bloom. (In hot-summer areas, sow this cool-loving plant in late summer to early fall for spring bloom.) Scatter the fine seed over the soil and rake it in lightly. Thin seedlings to stand about 6 inches (15 cm) apart.

LANDSCAPE USES: Plant Iceland poppies for early color in beds and borders; follow them with summer-blooming annuals. Grow some in the cutting garden, too, for fresh cut flowers. Harvest the stems in the morning, when the bud is facing upright but not yet open. Singe the stem ends in a gas flame or dip them in boiling water to prolong their vase life.

Corn poppy is a hardy annual grown for its summer flowers. Remove spent blooms at the base of the stem to extend the flowering season through most of the summer.

OTHER COMMON NAMES: Flanders poppy, Shirley poppy.

DESCRIPTION: Plants form clumps of ferny, blue-green leaves. Bowl-shaped flowers with four silky, crinkled petals open from plump, hairy buds atop thin, hairy stems. The 2–4-inch (5–10 cm) wide summer blooms are most often a glowing scarlet. Shirley poppy is a strain that has been selected for single or double flowers in a wider range of colors, including white, pink, red, and bicolors.

HEIGHT AND SPREAD: Height 24–36 inches (60–90 cm); spread 6–8 inches (15–20 cm).

BEST SITE: Full sun; average, well-drained soil.

GROWING GUIDELINES: Corn poppy is rewardingly easy to grow from seed sown directly into the garden in late fall or early spring. A second sowing in midspring can help extend the bloom season. Scatter the fine seed over the soil surface, then rake it in lightly. Thin seedlings to stand 6–8 inches (15–20 cm) apart. Leave a few flowers at the end of the season and plants will self-sow.

LANDSCAPE USES: Corn poppies are natural choices for adding sparkle to meadow gardens. They also look good as fillers in beds and borders, and the flowers are nice in arrangements, too. Pick them just as the buds are starting to open, then sear the ends of cut stems in a gas flame or dip them in boiling water to prolong their vase life.

Pelargonium x *hortorum*   Geraniaceae

ZONAL GERANIUM

Colorful and dependable, zonal geraniums are a mainstay of summer flower gardens. You can also bring them indoors in the fall and enjoy their flowers through the winter.

To keep your geraniums blooming, cut or snap off the stem of spent flower clusters where it joins the plant, before the long, narrow seedpods form.

DESCRIPTION: These tender perennials are usually grown as tender annuals for their attractive leaves and colorful flowers. The sturdy, branched stems carry hairy, rounded, bright to dark green leaves with scalloped margins. The pungent leaves are often marked with dark green or brown, curved bands (zones). Plants produce thin but sturdy stems topped with rounded clusters of many 2-inch (5 cm) wide flowers. The single or double flowers bloom from late spring until frost in white or shades of pink, red, salmon, and bicolors.

HEIGHT AND SPREAD: Height usually 12–24 inches (30–60 cm); spread usually 12–18 inches (30–45 cm).

BEST SITE: Full sun to partial shade; average, well-drained soil.

GROWING GUIDELINES: Zonal geraniums are a staple spring crop for most greenhouses and garden centers. If you just need a few geraniums or if you want special kinds (such as those with double flowers or fancy leaves), start with a few purchased plants in spring. Some kinds of zonal geraniums will also grow from seed. Sow the seed indoors 8–10 weeks before your last frost date. Plant it ⅛ inch (3 mm) deep. Set the pot in a very warm place (75°–80°F/24°–27°C) until seedlings appear, then move it to normal room temperature on a sunny windowsill or under lights. Separate the seedlings and move them to individual pots when they're large enough to handle.

Set plants out after the last frost date, when the soil is warm. If you plan to bring the plants inside for the winter, consider leaving them in their pots when you set them into the soil; then you can lift the plants easily in fall. Space plants 12–18 inches (30–45 cm) apart. During the summer, pinch off spent flower stems to promote rebloom. Plants may stop blooming during hot, humid spells but usually recover when cooler weather returns. To save special plants for next year, dig them up in fall, move them into pots, and grow them on a sunny windowsill. Take 4-inch (10 cm) long cuttings from the shoot tips in spring, insert them halfway into pots of moist potting soil, and set them in a warm, bright place. They should root in about 4 weeks. Move the rooted cuttings to the garden after the last frost date.

LANDSCAPE USES: Zonal geraniums are among the most versatile flowering annuals. Grow them alone in masses, or tuck them into beds and borders with other annuals and perennials as accents or fillers. Geraniums are great in container gardens, hanging baskets, and window boxes as well.

CULTIVARS: Many cultivars are available in a wide range of heights and colors. Plants in the seed-raised 'Orbit' series have zoned leaves on well-branched, 12–18-inch (30–45 cm) tall stems;

ZONAL GERANIUM—Continued

PETUNIA

Some cultivars have colored leaves that are even more striking than the flowers. In fact, you may want to cut off the blooms if you feel that they detract from the leaves.

Petunias are tender perennials usually grown as half-hardy annuals. They may self-sow, but the seedlings seldom resemble the parent plants.

they bloom in white and shades of red, pink, and orange. 'Apple Blossom Orbit' is a selection with light and dark pink blooms. Plants in the 'Elite' series have large flower heads in a mix of white, pinks, and reds on compact, 8–10-inch (20–25 cm) tall plants. 'Big Red' has large, scarlet flower clusters on 14-inch (35 cm) tall stems. 'Ben Franklin' has white-edged leaves and semidouble, magenta-pink blooms; it is raised from cuttings.

OTHER SPECIES:

P. graveolens, rose geranium, is grown for its scented, lobed leaves. It is a parent of many other wonderful scented geraniums; all are great for containers, flower beds, and herb gardens.

P. peltatum, ivy geranium, has lobed leaves and domed flower clusters in a range of reds and pinks on trailing stems. It is excellent for hanging baskets. Buy plants or grow from seed.

P. tomentosum, peppermint geranium, has broad, fuzzy, mint-scented leaves; it prefers partial shade.

DESCRIPTION: Plants form clumps of upright or trailing stems with oval, green leaves; both the leaves and stems are hairy and somewhat sticky. Funnel-shaped, single or double flowers bloom from early summer until frost in nearly every color of the rainbow; some have stripes, streaks, or bands of contrasting colors. Petunias are usually divided into groups, based on their flower forms. Grandifloras have the largest flowers (up to 4 or 5 inches [10–12.5 cm] across). They are very showy but tend to be damaged easily by heavy rain. Multifloras have smaller flowers (usually 2 inches [5 cm] across) but produce many durable blooms on each plant. Floribundas are an intermediate type, with 3-inch (7.5 cm) wide flowers on fast-growing plants.

HEIGHT AND SPREAD: Height usually 6–10 inches (15–25 cm); spread to 12 inches (30 cm).

BEST SITE: Full sun (can take light shade); average to moist, well-drained soil.

GROWING GUIDELINES: Petunias are among the most popular annuals, and many types are sold as transplants each spring. You can also grow your own from seed, although the fine, dust-like seed can be hard to handle. If you want to try, sow the seed indoors 8–10 weeks before your last frost date. Don't cover the seed; just press it lightly into the soil and enclose the pot in a plastic bag until

SCARLET RUNNER BEAN

To keep your petunias bushy and free-flowering, shear them back by one-third, water thoroughly, and fertilize after the first flush of blooms.

Scarlet runner beans are equally at home in the flower garden and the vegetable garden. The fast-growing vines produce showy orange-red blooms and edible seedpods.

seedlings appear. Move plants to the garden 1–2 weeks after the last frost date; space them 8–12 inches (20–30 cm) apart. Water during dry spells.

LANDSCAPE USES: Petunias—especially the multiflora and floribunda types—are favorites for flower beds and borders, planted alone in masses or mixed with other plants. They are particularly good for filling in gaps left by spring-flowering annuals and bulbs. Grandiflora types look great spilling out of containers, hanging baskets, and window boxes. The stems tend to drop their bottom leaves by late summer, so combine them with other bushy plants that will cover their bare ankles.

CULTIVARS: Petunias are available in an amazing range of flower forms and colors. Just a few of the dozens of available cultivars are covered here. Plants in the 'Resisto' series are multifloras with masses of single flowers on compact, bushy plants. 'Celebrity Mixed' is a long-flowering, floribunda type that grows quickly from seed and blooms in a range of colors. 'Fluffy Ruffles Mixed' has large, grandiflora-type flowers with wavy, crinkled edges. 'Summer Sun' has small, yellow flowers. 'Blue Daddy' has large purple-blue flowers with deep purple veining.

DESCRIPTION: This tender perennial climber is grown as a half-hardy annual. The twining stems carry broad, green, compound leaves with three leaflets. Showy clusters of 1-inch (2.5 cm) long, orange-red flowers bloom from midsummer until frost. The pea-like flowers are followed by long, silvery green pods that are quite tasty, especially when young (cook them like snap beans).

HEIGHT AND SPREAD: Height usually 6–8 feet (1.8–2.4 m); ultimate height and spread depend on the size of the support that scarlet runner bean is growing on.

BEST SITE: Full sun; average, well-drained soil.

GROWING GUIDELINES: Before planting, make sure you have a sturdy support such as a fence or stout posts already in place. This fast-growing vine is easy to start from seed sown directly into the garden. Wait until 1–2 weeks after the frost date, when the soil is warm; then plant the seed 1 inch (2.5 cm) deep. Thin seedlings to stand 8 inches (20 cm) apart. Water during dry spells.

LANDSCAPE USES: Scarlet runner bean is a good vine to grow as a screen for quick shade or privacy. It makes a super garden accent when trained to grow up a tripod of sturdy posts. It's also excellent as a temporary solution for covering an ugly section of fence or screening an unpleasant view.

ANNUAL PHLOX

Annual phlox is a hardy annual grown for its colorful flowers. If plants stop blooming, cut them back by half and water thoroughly; they should resprout and rebloom in fall.

DESCRIPTION: Plants form bushy clumps of narrow, lance-shaped, green leaves. From midsummer to fall, the leafy stems are topped with clusters of flat, five-petaled flowers, each ½–1 inch (12–25 mm) across. The flowers bloom in a wide range of colors, including white, pink, red, pale yellow, blue, and purple; some have a contrasting eye.

HEIGHT AND SPREAD: Height 6–18 inches (15–45 cm), depending on the cultivar; spread 6–8 inches (15–20 cm).

BEST SITE: Full sun; average, well-drained soil.

GROWING GUIDELINES: For the earliest flowers, buy transplants in spring, or grow your own by starting seed indoors 6–8 weeks before the last frost date. Sow seed ⅛ inch (3 mm) deep in individual pots. Set plants out around the last frost date. You can also sow seed directly into the garden around the last frost date. Set plants or thin seedlings to stand 6 inches (15 cm) apart. Pinching off spent flowers and watering during dry spells can prolong the bloom season.

LANDSCAPE USES: An excellent filler for flower beds and borders. Try the compact cultivars in container gardens and window boxes. Tall-stemmed cultivars are excellent as cut flowers, so grow some in the cutting garden.

CULTIVARS: 'Dwarf Beauty Mixed' blooms in a range of colors on compact, 6-inch (15 cm) tall plants.

ROSE MOSS

Rose moss comes in many vibrant colors, including white, pink, red, orange, yellow, and magenta. The flowers tend to close by afternoon and stay closed on cloudy days.

DESCRIPTION: A low-growing, tender annual, rose moss forms creeping mats of fleshy, reddish, many-branched stems with small, thick, almost needle-like leaves. Single or double, 1-inch (2.5 cm) wide flowers bloom from early summer through fall.

HEIGHT AND SPREAD: Height to 6 inches (15 cm); spread 6–8 inches (15–20 cm).

BEST SITE: Full sun; average, well-drained to dry soil.

GROWING GUIDELINES: For earliest bloom, buy transplants in spring, or start your own by sowing seed indoors 6–8 weeks before your last frost date. For easy transplanting later, sow the seed in cell packs or small pots. Do not cover the seed; just press it lightly into the soil and enclose the containers in a **plastic bag until seedlings appear. Set plants out 1-2 weeks after the last frost date, when the soil is warm; space them about 6 inches (15 cm) apart. You can also sow the fine seed directly into the garden after the last frost date; keep the soil moist until seedlings appear. Thin seedlings only if they're crowded. Established plants may self-sow.**

LANDSCAPE USES: Makes a great groundcover for dry, rocky slopes. It also looks charming as an edging for sunny beds and borders or cascading out of containers and hanging baskets.

CULTIVARS: 'Cloudbeater Mixed' grows to 6 inches (15 cm) tall and has double flowers that stay open all day.

Ricinus communis Euphorbiaceae	*Rudbeckia hirta* Compositae

CASTOR BEAN

BLACK-EYED SUSAN

Castor beans add a touch of the tropics to any garden. Stake the tall plants to keep them upright, especially in windy or exposed sites, and water them during dry spells.

The daisy-like blooms of black-eyed Susans have golden yellow outer petals and a purple-brown or black, raised center. They make excellent cut flowers.

OTHER COMMON NAMES: Gloriosa daisy.

DESCRIPTION: This tender perennial is usually grown as a half-hardy annual. The huge, fast-growing plants produce thick, sturdy stems with large, deeply lobed, green or purplish brown leaves. Small, ½-inch (12 mm) wide, creamy-looking, petal-less flowers bloom in spiky clusters along the upper part of the stems. These summer flowers are followed by showy, spiny, reddish burs.

HEIGHT AND SPREAD: Height usually to 6 feet (1.8 m) or more; spread 3–4 feet (90–120 cm).

BEST SITE: Full sun; average to moist, well-drained soil.

GROWING GUIDELINES: For an early start, sow seed indoors 6–8 weeks before your last frost date. Soak the large, speckled seeds in warm water overnight, then sow seed ¾ inch (18 mm) deep in individual pots (two or three seeds per pot). If all of the seeds germinate, thin to one per pot. Set plants out 1-2 weeks after the last frost date. You can also sow seed directly into the garden after the last frost date. Space plants or thin seedlings to stand about 3 feet (90 cm) apart. Plants may self-sow.

LANDSCAPE USES: Grow castor beans as accents or backgrounds for beds and borders or as a temporary but fast-growing screen or hedge. The seeds are poisonous if eaten, so avoid planting castor beans around children's play areas.

CULTIVARS: 'Carmencita' has brownish leaves and bright red seedpods on 6-foot (1.8 m) tall plants.

DESCRIPTION: This short-lived perennial or biennial is usually grown as a hardy annual. Plants form clumps of long, hairy leaves that taper to a point. Stiff, hairy stems are topped with 2–3-inch (5–7.5 cm) wide flowers from summer into fall.

HEIGHT AND SPREAD: Height 24–36 inches (60–90 cm); spread to about 12 inches (30 cm).

BEST SITE: Full sun (can take light shade); average, well-drained to dry soil.

GROWING GUIDELINES: For earliest bloom, sow seed indoors 8–10 weeks before your last frost date. Just barely cover the seed. Set plants out 1-2 weeks before the last frost date (protect plants if there's a chance of heavy frost). You can also sow seed directly into the garden after the last frost date, although those plants probably won't bloom until the following year. Space plants or thin seedlings to stand 12 inches (30 cm) apart. Plants often self-sow; if this is a problem, remove spent flowers before they set seed.

LANDSCAPE USES: Black-eyed Susans look bright and cheerful in flower beds and borders. They're also a natural choice for meadow gardens.

CULTIVARS: 'Gloriosa Daisy' includes tetraploid forms that have large single, semidouble, or double flowers. They bloom in yellow, orange, brown, and reddish brown, on 24–36-inch (60–90 cm) stems.

| *Salvia farinacea* | Labiatae | *Salvia splendens* | Labiatae |

MEALY-CUP SAGE

SCARLET SAGE

Mealy-cup sage is fairly drought-tolerant but appreciates watering during extended spells. The plants sometimes live through mild winters; they may also self-sow.

Compact cultivars of scarlet sage tend to flower mostly in summer; taller types generally start blooming in midsummer and last until frost. Pinch off faded spikes.

OTHER COMMON NAMES: Blue salvia.

DESCRIPTION: This tender perennial is usually grown as a half-hardy annual. Plants produce bushy clumps of narrow, lance-shaped, green leaves with slightly toothed edges. Stiff, purple-blue stem tips are topped with long spikes of dusty blue buds from midsummer until frost. These buds open to ½-inch (12 mm) long, blue flowers.

HEIGHT AND SPREAD: Height usually 18–24 inches (45–60 cm); spread to 12 inches (30 cm).

BEST SITE: Full sun; average, well-drained soil.

GROWING GUIDELINES: Buy transplants in spring, or grow your own by starting seed indoors 8–10 weeks before your last frost date. Soaking the seed overnight before planting can promote quicker sprouting. Don't cover the sown seed; just press it lightly into the soil and enclose the pot in a plastic bag until seedlings appear. Set plants out after the last frost date; space them 12 inches (30 cm) apart.

LANDSCAPE USES: Looks marvelous alone in masses or mixed with other annuals, perennials, and roses in beds, borders, and cottage gardens. The neat, shrubby plants are ideal for containers, too. The spiky blooms are useful for fresh or dried arrangements, so grow some plants in the cutting garden.

CULTIVARS: 'Victoria' has deep blue flowers on 18-inch (45 cm) tall plants. 'White Porcelain' has white flowers on 18-inch (45 cm) tall plants.

DESCRIPTION: This tender perennial is grown as a half-hardy annual. Plants form clumps of upright stems with oval, deep green leaves that have pointed tips and slightly toothed edges. The stems are topped with thick, showy spikes of colorful, petal-like bracts and 1½-inch (37 mm) long, tubular flowers. The flowers are most often red, but they are also available in white, pink, salmon, and purple.

HEIGHT AND SPREAD: Height usually 12–24 inches (30–60 cm); spread to 12 inches (30 cm).

BEST SITE: Full sun; average, well-drained soil.

GROWING GUIDELINES: Widely sold as transplants in spring. If you really want to grow your own, sow indoors 8–10 weeks before your last frost date. Don't cover the seed; just press it lightly into the soil and enclose the pot in a plastic bag until seedlings appear. Set plants out after the last frost date; space them 8–12 inches (20–30 cm) apart. Fertilize several times during the summer.

LANDSCAPE USES: If you enjoy mixing bright colors, grow scarlet sage as an edging or filler for flower beds and borders. For a somewhat more restrained effect, surround scarlet sage with leafy green herbs and ornamental grasses.

CULTIVARS: 'Bonfire' blooms with scarlet flowers on 24-inch (60 cm) tall plants from midsummer until frost. 'Laser Purple' grows to 12 inches (30 cm) tall and has deep purple flowers.

Sanvitalia procumbens   Compositae

CREEPING ZINNIA

Plant creeping zinnia where it can trail over walls, or allow it to cascade out of containers, raised beds, window boxes, and hanging baskets.

DESCRIPTION: Creeping zinnia is usually grown as a half-hardy annual for its colorful flowers. Plants form spreading or trailing mounds of branching stems and oval green leaves that taper to a point. The mounds are covered with many ¾-inch (18 mm) wide flowers that resemble miniature black-eyed Susans from midsummer until frost. The raised, purple-brown centers are surrounded by a ring of golden yellow petals.

HEIGHT AND SPREAD: Height to 6 inches (15 cm); spread to 18 inches (45 cm).

BEST SITE: Full sun; average, well-drained to dry soil.

GROWING GUIDELINES: For earliest bloom, sow seed indoors 6–8 weeks before your last frost date. Sow in individual pots so you won't have to disturb the roots at transplanting time. Don't cover the fine seed; just press it lightly into the soil and enclose the pots in a plastic bag until seedlings appear. Set plants out after the last frost date. You can also sow seed directly into the garden after the last frost date. Space plants or thin seedlings to stand 8–12 inches (20–30 cm) apart. Established plants are care-free.

LANDSCAPE USES: Creeping zinnia makes a great groundcover in dry, sunny spots. It's also useful as an edging or filler for flower beds and borders.

CULTIVARS: 'Mandarin Orange' has orange flowers on 6-inch (15 cm) tall plants.

Senecio cineraria   Compositae

DUSTY MILLER

Dusty miller can live through mild winters, but second-year plants tend to be more open. Where uniformity is important (as in an edging), start with new plants each year.

DESCRIPTION: This tender perennial is usually grown as a half-hardy annual. Plants form shrubby mounds of deeply lobed leaves that are covered with matted, white hairs. The plants may produce clusters of daisy-like yellow flowers in summer, but these are usually removed so they won't detract from the silvery foliage. Dusty miller is also listed in seed catalogs as *Cineraria maritima*.

HEIGHT AND SPREAD: Height 8–24 inches (20–60 cm); spread to 12 inches (30 cm).

BEST SITE: Full sun; average, well-drained soil.

GROWING GUIDELINES: Transplants are easy to find for purchase in spring. They grow slowly from seed, but if you want to raise your own, sow seed indoors 8–10 weeks before your last frost date. Don't cover the seed; just press it lightly into the soil and enclose the pot in a plastic bag until seedlings appear. Set plants out after the last frost date; space them 8 inches (20 cm) apart. Pinch out stem tips in early summer to promote bushy growth.

LANDSCAPE USES: Dusty miller's silvery foliage is invaluable as an edging or accent for flower beds, borders, and all kinds of container plantings. The silvery leaves and stems also dry well. (For drying, bundle stems in small bunches and hang them upside down in a dark, airy place.)

CULTIVARS: 'Silver Dust' grows to 8 inches (20 cm) tall and has finely cut, silver-white leaves.

MARIGOLDS

Marigolds can add bright color to any sunny spot. Mix them with other annuals and perennials, or grow them alone in masses. Tall-stemmed types may need staking.

The fragrant, ferny foliage of signet marigold is topped by masses of small flowers. Grow it as you would other marigolds. The plants are great for edging beds and borders.

DESCRIPTION: These popular half-hardy annuals are grown for their bright, 2–4-inch (5–10 cm) wide summer flowers and bushy mounds of lacy, green leaves. African or American marigolds (*T. erecta*) tend to be large plants, with 18–36-inch (45–90 cm) stems and large, usually double, yellow or orange flowers. French marigolds (*T. patula*) tend to be much daintier, with many smaller, single or double flowers in yellow, orange, or red on 12-inch (30 cm) tall plants. There are also hybrids between the two species. The seeds of these triploid hybrids tend to have a low germination rate, and some of those that do sprout may produce tall, coarse plants that need to be removed so they won't detract from the others. On the good side, though, these hybrids don't set seed, so their flowers last longer. They are also quite heat-tolerant.

HEIGHT AND SPREAD: Height 6–36 inches (15–90 cm); spread 6–18 inches (15–45 cm).

BEST SITE: Full sun; average, well-drained soil. Light afternoon shade can help prolong bloom in hot-summer areas, especially for creamy-flowered cultivars.

GROWING GUIDELINES: It is quite easy to grow your own marigolds from seed. For earliest bloom (especially for tall-growing types), start seed indoors 4–6 weeks before your last frost date. Plant seed ⅛–¼ inch (3–6 mm) deep. Set plants out after your last frost date. You can also sow seed of small, early-blooming types directly into the garden after the last frost date. Space plants or thin seedlings of dwarf types to stand 6–8 inches (15–20 cm) apart; leave 12–18 inches (30–45 cm) between larger cultivars. Pinch off spent blooms weekly to prolong the bloom season. Plants may self-sow.

LANDSCAPE USES: Grow marigolds as summer fillers or edgings for flower beds, borders, and containers. They also last well in fresh arrangements, so include a few in the cutting garden. (If you don't like the pungent scent of most marigold flowers, try growing an odorless cultivar instead.) Use the tall-stemmed kinds as a flowering hedge.

CULTIVARS: 'Disco Mixed' is a compact, early-blooming French cultivar with single, gold, orange, red, and red-and-gold flowers on 6-inch (15 cm) tall plants. 'Climax Mixed' is an African type with big, double, orange or yellow flowers on 36-inch (90 cm) tall plants. 'French Vanilla Hybrid' is an African type with odorless, creamy white flowers on 24-inch (60 cm) tall plants. 'Nugget Supreme Mixed' is a triploid hybrid that grows to 12 inches (30 cm) tall and has yellow, gold, orange, or red double flowers.

OTHER SPECIES:

T. tenuifolia, signet marigold, forms 6–12-inch (15–30 cm) tall mounds of ferny, lemon-scented leaves and small, single, yellow or orange flowers.

| *Thunbergia alata* Acanthaceae | *Tithonia rotundifolia* Compositae |

BLACK-EYED SUSAN VINE

MEXICAN SUNFLOWER

If you plan to grow black-eyed Susan vine as a climber, install some type of support—such as plastic netting or a trellis—before planting.

OTHER COMMON NAMES: Clock vine.

DESCRIPTION: This tender perennial is grown as a tender annual. Plants produce twining vines with heart- to arrowhead-shaped, green leaves. Pointed buds open to rounded, flattened, 3-inch (7.5 cm) wide flowers. The orange-yellow flowers have a deep purple to black center. They may bloom from late summer until frost, but they usually put on their best show in late summer to early fall.

HEIGHT AND SPREAD: Height to about 6 feet (1.8 m); ultimate height and spread depend on the support the vine is growing on.

BEST SITE: Full sun to partial shade; average to moist, well-drained soil.

GROWING GUIDELINES: For earliest flowers, start seed indoors 6–8 weeks before your last frost date. Sow seed ¼ inch (6 mm) deep in peat pots (two or three seeds per pot); thin to leave one seedling per pot. Set plants out 1-2 weeks after the last frost date. You can also start plants from seed sown directly into the garden after the last frost date. Set plants or thin seedlings to stand 12 inches (30 cm) apart. Mulch plants to keep the roots cool. Water during dry spells.

LANDSCAPE USES: Black-eyed Susan vine is a good fast-growing screen for shade or privacy. It also makes a unique feature in a hanging basket, where it will climb up the support wires to create a pyramid of foliage and flowers.

Mexican sunflowers are popular with bees and butterflies, and they make good cut flowers. Pinch off spent blooms to extend the flowering season.

OTHER COMMON NAMES: Torch flower.

DESCRIPTION: Mexican sunflower is a half-hardy annual with colorful blooms. Plants produce tall, sturdy, hairy stems with velvety, lobed or broadly oval, pointed, dark green leaves. During summer, the shrubby clumps are accented with many 3-inch (7.5 cm) wide, glowing orange, daisy-like flowers.

HEIGHT AND SPREAD: Height 4–6 feet (1.2–1.8 m); spread 18–24 inches (45–60 cm).

BEST SITE: Full sun; average, well-drained soil with added organic matter.

GROWING GUIDELINES: For earliest flowers, start seed indoors 6–8 weeks before your last frost date. Sow seed ¼ inch (6 mm) deep in individual pots (two or three seeds per pot); thin to leave one seedling per pot. Set plants out after the last frost date. Mexican sunflowers also grow quickly and easily from seed sown directly into the garden about 2 weeks after the last frost date. Set plants or thin seedlings to stand 18 inches (45 cm) apart. Water during dry spells. Plants growing in exposed sites may need staking.

LANDSCAPE USES: Makes an attractive flowering screen or hedge. It also looks great as a tall accent or background plant in beds and borders.

CULTIVARS: 'Torch' has orange flowers on 4–6-foot (1.2–1.8 m) tall stems. 'Yellow Torch' grows to 4 feet (1.2 m) tall and has bright yellow flowers.

BULBS IN YOUR GARDEN

Beautiful and versatile, bulbs belong in every landscape. Many popular bulbs—including daffodils, crocus, hyacinths, and tulips—are traditionally associated with spring gardens. But with a little planning, you can have bulbs in bloom in your garden from late winter through midfall. And to fill the few months that bulbs aren't blooming outdoors, you can bring some kinds indoors and enjoy their colorful flowers all winter long.

In this chapter, you'll find great ideas on gardening with bulbs throughout the year. Celebrate surviving another long winter with colorful displays of crocus, daffodils, and other dependable, easy-care bulbs; you'll discover lots of planting tips and combination suggestions in "Bulbs for Spring" on page 106. Spice up your summer gardens with the easy-but-elegant plants covered in "Bulbs for Summer" on page 110. And extend the season with lovely late bloomers, such as showy crocus (*Crocus speciosus*) and hardy cyclamen (*Cyclamen hederifolium*); you'll learn about their planting and care needs in "Bulbs for Fall" on page 112.

If three seasons of bloom aren't enough for you, try "forcing" some of your bulbs to have flowers indoors in winter. In "Bulbs for Indoor Bloom" on page 114, you'll find basic forcing techniques for dependable bulbs and tips for displaying and maintaining them to have the blooms look their best.

While you're enjoying your forced bulbs indoors, take some time to plan where you can add more outdoor bulbs to your garden. "Bulbs and Companions" on page 116 is full of inspiring ideas on mixing bulbs with annuals, perennials, groundcovers, shrubs, and other plants. See "Bulbs for Container Gardens" on page 118 for pointers on growing bulbs in pots for spots of portable color. Liven up your lawn and low-maintenance areas with mass plantings of crocus and other small bulbs; see "Bulbs for Naturalizing" on page 120 for complete details. And if you enjoy having fresh flowers for indoor arrangements, don't forget that bulbs are great for cutting! See "Bulbs for Cutting Gardens" on page 122 for guidelines on choosing, growing, and gathering the best bulb blooms.

Bulb blooms come in a range of rich hues and delicate pastels, allowing them to blend beautifully into any garden planting. Besides hyacinths and other spring favorites, you can grow summer- and fall-flowering bulbs, too.

The beautifully shaped blooms and spiky foliage of reticulated irises may appear even before the last of the snow has melted.

Different tulip cultivars bloom at different times, so you can enjoy them all through the spring.

Bulbs for Spring

Many gardeners have a special affection for spring-flowering bulbs. These early-blooming beauties signal the return of life to the garden after the rigors of a long, cold winter, adding welcome color and fragrance to any planting.

Bulbs from around the world have found a home in American gardens, despite our wide diversity of climate conditions. Most of the best-beloved bulbs—including daffodils and crocus—have earned their popularity because of their ability to adapt to a wide variety of growing conditions. Not all bulbs thrive in all parts of the country, but there are at least a few beautiful spring bulbs for virtually every area.

How Spring Bulbs Grow

Spring-flowering bulbs are best adapted to temperate areas, where they can take advantage of a particular weather "window." These bulbs send up shoots early in the season—sometimes before winter has finally relinquished its icy grasp. Melting snow and ample spring rain provide a good supply of moisture as the bulbs send up their buds, hoping to attract the first bees and other insects to ensure pollination. Even though the ground is still cool, the lengthening rays of sunshine provide enough warmth to promote bloom. As summer approaches the days get longer and the bulbs set seed and ripen their foliage, preparing to end this part of their life cycle.

By the time summer's heat arrives—often accompanied by a drop in rainfall—the bulbs are plump and moist and packed with stored nutrients. Their leaves wither away, their seed drops to the ground, and the bulbs become dormant for the summer.

As fall returns, it brings cooler temperatures and increased rainfall—conditions that encourage the bulbs to start growing again. The still-warm ground provides great conditions for root growth, while increasingly colder temperatures generally discourage the bulbs

The daisy-like blooms of Grecian windflowers are a welcome sight in spring. They are easy to grow and will spread.

from making much topgrowth. As spring arrives once again, the warm sun triggers the bounty of blossoms that we anticipate so eagerly.

Little but Lovely Early Bulbs

In much of the nation, the first flowering bulbs often jump the gun and bloom in late winter. These little treasures are often called "minor" bulbs because of their small stature compared to taller tulips, hyacinths, and daffodils. But even though they're small in size, they're big on charm and all the more welcome due to their early appearance in the garden.

Snowdrops (*Galanthus nivalis*) and spring snowflakes (*Leucojum vernum*) often arrive first. Their white petals, tinged with green, dangle just a few inches above the warming soil. The flowers of spring snowflake have three separate "petals" that dangle from thin stems, while the flowers on snowdrops resemble tiny inflated parachutes. Winter aconite (*Eranthis hyemalis*) blooms at about the same time, with short-stemmed, golden yellow flowers surrounded by a collar of frilled leaves.

Like the other early bloomers, snow crocus (*Crocus chrysanthus*) thrives in the brisk weather of late winter and early spring. It flowers in shades of yellow, lavender, and white. Its larger cousin, the plump hybrid Dutch crocus (*C. vernus*), blooms a few weeks later. It bears beautiful chalice-shaped blooms in lustrous shades of violet, lavender, and white, some with striking markings or stripes on the satiny petals.

Grecian windflower (*Anemone blanda*) displays a totally different look from other early-blooming bulbs, with many-petaled, daisy-like flowers and parsley-like

'February Gold' daffodils produce dainty, nodding flowers in very early spring. Pair them with evergreens for extra interest.

leaves. It opens wide under sunny skies, with showy pink, white, or Wedgwood blue petals.

Snow irises produce thin, spear-like leaves and graceful flowers equal in beauty to their larger summer-blooming relatives. Among the most commonly grown snow irises are *Iris danfordiae*, with yellow flowers, and reticulated iris (*I. reticulata*) and *I. histrioides*, which

Grape hyacinths may produce some leaves in fall, but spring is the time to enjoy the clustered blooms.

Some Like It Cool

Winter chilling is an important step in the life of most spring-blooming bulbs. If you live in a warm climate, where winter temperatures generally stay above freezing, you may find that some spring bulbs bloom poorly or don't bloom at all in the years after planting. Hybrid tulips commonly have this problem; some daffodils and crocus also grow poorly without a chilling period.

To have a great show of blooms each year, look for species and cultivars that don't need much chilling. (Ask your neighbors, local garden centers, or Cooperative Extension Service to recommend the bulbs that grow best in your area.) You can also look for "precooled" bulbs, or give new bulbs an artificial cold period by storing them in the vegetable drawer of your refrigerator for 6 to 8 weeks before planting them in early- to mid-winter.

bloom in shades of blue, purple, and wine-red.

Additional small spring charmers include Siberian squill (*Scilla sibirica*), striped squill (*Puschkinia scilloides*), and glory-of-the-snow (*Chionodoxa luciliae*). Siberian squill is valued for its pendant, royal blue flowers that bloom on short 4- to 6-inch (10 to 15 cm) tall stalks; a white form ('Alba') is also available. Striped squill has milky white petals, each with a stripe of turquoise blue. Glory-of-the-snow has star-shaped flowers in pink, blue, or lavender-blue, often with a white eye in the center of each bloom.

Of course, you can't forget to include grape hyacinth (*Muscari armeniacum*), an old-fashioned favorite treasured for its crowded spikes of rounded flowers that resemble tiny grapes. The blue, pink, or white, bell-shaped blooms of wood hyacinth (*Hyacinthoides hispanica*) are also delightful in lightly shaded gardens.

Showy Spring Standbys

The early-spring show of minor bulbs sets the stage for the most spectacular spring-flowering favorites, including daffodils, hyacinths, tulips, and crown imperials (*Fritillaria imperialis*).

Let's face it—spring just wouldn't be spring without daffodils. Sometimes referred to as jonquils, daffodils belong to the genus *Narcissus*. With hundreds of species and perhaps thousands of hybrids and cultivars, the variations on the standard yellow, large-cupped daffodil are almost endless. Some types are best

Create a sea of spring color by planting some crocus in your lawn. Wait to mow until the crocus leaves have yellowed.

suited for Southern gardens, while others prefer cooler climates. There are types that bear a single flower on each stem and those that produce clusters of blooms. The stems themselves range in size from just a few inches (7.5 to 10 cm) tall to nearly 2 feet (60 cm) tall. For extra interest, consider the variety of single and double flower forms and the range of colors (including yellow, cream, white, chartreuse, and bicolors). You'll see that there's a perfect daffodil for nearly every garden spot. As a plus, most daffodils have a light scent, and many have distinct, powerful fragrances.

Of course, when you're thinking about fragrant spring bulbs, you can't forget the heady scent of hybrid

Bluebells (*Hyacinthoides* spp.) can reseed prolifically to produce large patches. Give them a site where they can spread, or mow off the seedpods to prevent reseeding.

Winter aconites add bright spring color to borders and woodlands.

Create a pretty spring picture by pairing snowdrops (*Galanthus* spp.) with Italian arum (*Arum italicum*).

hyacinths (*Hyacinthus orientalis*). The impressive flower spikes, packed with many small blooms, usually grow 6 to 10 inches (15 to 25 cm) tall. Hyacinths come in a wide range of colors, including white, blue, pink, coral, and pale yellow. Double-flowered cultivars were popular in Victorian times and are enjoying a renewed wave of interest.

Along with daffodils and hyacinths, tulips are a spring-garden standby. Blooming in white and nearly every shade of red, pink, orange, yellow, and purple, hybrid tulips are only lacking true blue in the color department. Their flowers come in many forms, from the classic chalice shape to petal-packed doubles, exotically "feathered" parrot types, and elegant, pointed-petal lily types. Smaller-flowered and shorter "species" tulips are also great in the garden. Some tulips offer striped, mottled, or variegated leaves to complement their lovely blossoms. By choosing a range of cultivars with different bloom times and leaf patterns, you can enjoy tulips throughout the entire spring season.

If you're looking for something really distinctive to liven up your spring garden, consider planting a few bulbs of crown imperial (*Fritillaria imperalis*). The bottom half of its stiff stem is covered with whorls of narrow, bright green leaves; the upper half bears a crown of large, nodding flowers topped with a tuft of green leaves. The flowers are commonly orange, although the yellow

Special Care for Spring Bulbs

It's easy to add spring bulbs to your garden, but it does take a little advance planning. Mail-order catalogs of spring bulbs often arrive in spring to early summer, so you can decide what your garden needs and place your order for delivery in fall. Late summer and fall are also the times you'll find spring bulbs for sale at local garden centers. In Northern gardens, early- to mid-fall is the best time to plant; in Southern areas, the planting season continues through early winter. You'll find complete planting guidelines in "Planting Bulbs" on page 128.

Water spring bulbs just after planting and again as needed if the soil dries out in winter or spring. Scatter compost or balanced organic fertilizer over the soil when the new shoots appear in spring to provide a nutrient boost for healthy growth and good flower bud formation for next year.

Most spring bulbs thrive in full or partial sun (at least 6 hours of sun a day). They are ideal for planting under deciduous trees, since the bulbs can bloom and ripen their foliage before the tree leaves expand fully and block the sunlight. Unless you're planning to plant replacement bulbs each year (as you may with hybrid tulips), always allow the bulb leaves to wither away naturally. If you cut off, pull off, or bundle the leaves together, the bulb won't be able to store all the energy it needs, and it may bloom poorly or even die by the next year.

form is very popular. The plants bear a strange odor—sometimes likened to the scent of foxes—that is distasteful to some people. For this reason, you may want to plant crown imperials away from your house so you and your visitors can enjoy looking at them without having to smell them all the time. Some gardeners claim that the smell discourages rodents in a garden.

Bulbs for Summer

Don't think the bulb season is over when the last spring blossom fades! The tulips may be just a memory, but there are many more beautiful blossoms ahead.

Ornamental Onions

While onions, garlic, and leeks are staples of the vegetable garden, ornamental onions are a mainstay of the early-summer flower garden. The most impressive of the ornamental onions is giant onion (*Allium giganteum*). Its strong flower stems—up to 4 feet (1.2 m) tall—are topped with grapefruit-sized globes of tightly packed purple flowers in early summer. Persian onion (*A. aflatunense*) is slightly smaller but also quite showy, with softball-sized clusters of lavender-purple flowers on 3-foot (90 cm) tall stems.

Other popular early-summer ornamental onions include star of Persia (*A. christophii*), drumstick chives (*A. sphaerocephalum*), and lily leek (*A. moly*). Star of Persia grows 10 to 24 inches (25 to 60 cm) tall and has cantaloupe-sized heads of starry, pale violet flowers. Drumstick chives has tight, oval-shaped, maroon-red flower heads, not much bigger than a golf ball, on wiry stems from 2 to 4 feet (60 to 120 cm) tall. Lily leek offers a rather different look from the other ornamental onions, with small heads of yellow flowers in late spring or early summer on stems 8 to 14 inches (20–35 cm) tall.

Lovely Lilies

Lilies are the stars of the mid- to late-summer garden. True lilies (*Lilium* spp. and hybrids) grow from a bulb and have straight stems with many short leaves. Although their flower form resembles that of the daylily (*Hemerocallis* spp.), true lilies have individual blooms that can stay open for several weeks, as opposed to the one-day duration of a daylily blossom.

Hybrid lilies are divided into several broad groups. The three main groups are the Asiatic hybrids, trumpet lilies, and oriental hybrids. Asiatic hybrids are the first to bloom, flowering from late May into July in most parts of the country. They are noted for their large, beautifully colored and shaped flowers; most are not fragrant. July and August belong to the trumpet lilies (also known as Aurelian hybrids). They come in a more limited color range (mainly white, yellow, pink, and apricot), but their huge, horn-shaped blooms bear

Tuberous begonias are beautiful for baskets and pots, either alone or combined with other plants for even more color.

a sweet perfume. Fragrance is also a feature of the oriental hybrids, which bloom from midsummer into fall (depending on the cultivar). Their incredibly beautiful flowers bloom in white and shades of pink to cherry red, often with raised spots.

Great Gladioli

Gladioli are flower-garden favorites with spikes of satin-textured blooms in an almost infinite variety of colors—from pastel pink, white, and yellow to rich purple, orange, and magenta. Breeders have also created many bicolor types, with various degrees of petal ruffling and feathering. The showy flower spikes are super for cutting. And if you plant at 2-week intervals

Asiatic lilies are excellent for adding height to summer beds and borders. They are also wonderful as cut flowers.

If you're looking for something a little different, consider growing Turkestan onion (*Allium karataviense*). It looks great with other sun-loving, silvery plants.

Dahlias came in a range of heights and colors to accent any garden.

from midspring to midsummer, you can enjoy waves of blooms throughout the growing season.

Other Super Summer Bulbs

If you're looking for more bulbs to brighten up your summer garden, here are some super ones to try. To learn more about any of the bulbs listed below, check out their individual entry in the "Guide to Bulbs," starting on page 138.

Caladiums The bold, beautiful leaves of caladiums are ideal for accenting the summer shade garden. The fabulous white, green, or pink foliage is a real attention-getter, with prominent patterns and veining in contrasting shades of rose, red, and green.

Cannas Cannas produce clumps of broad, tropical-looking leaves, topped by clusters of brilliant flowers in pink, coral, red, orange, yellow, and bicolors. Cannas thrive in warm weather and can reach 10 feet (3 m) tall when they get plenty of water. (Dwarf types are also available.) Cannas are hardy in many parts of the South but need to be dug for indoor winter storage elsewhere.

Dahlias Dahlias are a signature plant of summer gardens across much of the country. These tender Mexican natives bloom best when the weather is hot and moist. They range in size from compact container plants to 5-foot (1.5 m) tall giants, with showy flowers in an amazing array of colors, sizes, and forms.

Tuberous Begonias Tuberous begonias thrive in partial shade and produce a long show of brilliant flowers during the heat of summer. Try upright types in shady beds and patio pots; allow cascading types to spill out of hanging baskets and window boxes.

Special Care for Summer Bulbs

Some summer bulbs—including lilies and ornamental onions (*Allium* spp.)—can live from year to year, so you'll plant them once and enjoy their blooms for years to come. These "hardy" bulbs are usually planted in fall for bloom the following summer, although lilies can also adapt to early-spring planting. The key is to plant early enough so the root system can get established before warm weather promotes lush topgrowth.

Other summer bloomers are classified as "tender" bulbs. These cold-sensitive beauties may not be able to survive the winter in your area. Unless you live in a warm climate (roughly Zone 8 and south), you'll need to plant gladioli, cannas, dahlias, and other tender bulbs in spring to early summer and dig them up in the fall for winter storage indoors. For more information, see "Handling Tender Bulbs" on page 134.

Bulbs for Fall

The end of summer doesn't spell the end of the bulb season. The fall show continues with holdovers from summer, such as dahlias, cannas, tuberous begonias, and some oriental lilies. These are complemented by bulbs that wait until the return of cold weather to bloom. The charm of fall-blooming bulbs is the grace and freshness they add to the late-season garden. They are wonderful companions for fall-flowering perennials, including asters, mums, and Japanese anemone (*Anemone* x *hybrida*). For extra interest, plant low-growing groundcovers, such as sedums, creeping veronicas (*Veronica* spp.), creeping Jenny (*Lysimachia nummularia*), and thyme, directly over the bulbs. As the bulbs bloom, the groundcover provides a leafy backdrop that is far more pleasing than bare soil.

To enjoy the beauty of fall bulbs in your own garden, try any or all of those discussed here.

Tall Fall Flowers

If you're looking to add some excitement to your late-season plantings, consider adding a few magic lilies (*Lycoris squamigera*) or naked ladies (*Amaryllis belladonna*) to your flower beds. Magic lilies, also known as surprise lilies, seem to appear out of nowhere in late summer to

Striking winter leaves, interesting spring flowers, and showy fall fruit give Italian arum multiseason interest.

early fall. They send up leafless, 2-foot (60 cm) tall stems topped with pale pink, lily-like flowers. The infamous naked lady has a similar habit and look but is less cold-hardy, growing best in Zones 7 to 9 (as compared to Zones 5 to 9 for magic lilies). Both plants produce leaves in spring and early summer; these leaves wither away a month or two before the flowering stems appear.

Italian arum (*Arum italicum*) is another dramatic addition to the garden. It is especially showy in fall, when it produces round, orange berries in clusters atop thick stems up to 18 inches (45 cm) tall. The berries are complemented by arrow-shaped green leaves that are often patterned with cream or white markings. The leaves emerge in fall, persist through the winter, and disappear in late spring. Italian arum also has hooded white flowers in spring, but the blooms are not nearly as spectacular as the fall berries.

Special Care for Fall Bulbs

Once you get them in the ground, fall-flowering bulbs are easy to grow. The trick is remembering to plant them at the right time of year. Magic lilies and naked ladies are best planted in early summer, when the bulbs are dormant. Late summer or early fall, just before their bloom starts, is the best time for most other fall-flowering bulbs.

Like other bulbs, fall bloomers need to ripen their leaves fully to store enough food for good flowering. So live with their leaves until they wither away—don't cut or pull them off before they turn yellow. If you "naturalize" fall bulbs in grassy areas, you'll also need to remember to stop mowing as soon as you see the first flower buds emerging from the soil in late summer to early fall.

Naked ladies (*Amaryllis belladonna*) and *Nerine bowdenii* ripen their leaves in spring but don't bloom until fall.

Showy crocus looks wonderful naturalized in grassy areas for fall bloom.

Combine fall bulbs with groundcovers, such as leadwort (*Ceratostigma plumbaginoides*), to help support the blooms and keep them clean.

Little Late Bloomers

Smaller fall-flowering bulbs are equally valuable for late-season interest. Start with some of the fall-blooming crocus, such as showy crocus (*Crocus speciosus*) and saffron crocus (*C. sativus*). Showy crocus braves the coolest weather of fall, opening its 6- to 8-inch (15 to 20 cm) tall, chalice-shaped flowers during sunny days. The petals are pale lavender with deeper purple stripes. Showy crocus leaves appear in spring and go dormant in summer. Saffron crocus, on the other hand, blooms with its leaves, which persist through winter and die back in spring. Saffron crocus is the source for the yellow spice, which is made from the dried stigmas (female flower parts). The flowers are similar in height and color to those of showy crocus.

Slightly larger than the true crocus, showy autumn crocus (*Colchicum speciosum*) emerge from the soil in September and October (in most parts of the country). Several cultivars and hybrids are available, blooming in pink, rosy lavender, and white; some have a pale checkered pattern on the petals. A double form called 'Waterlily' is lavender-pink and has many petals. The broad, strap-like leaves of showy autumn crocus appear in spring and die back to the ground in summer.

Hardy cyclamen (*Cyclamen hederifolium*) is another charming addition to any garden. In fall, its pink flowers flutter over the soil on stems up to 6 inches (15 cm) tall. The dark green leaves mottled with frosty silver emerge soon after the blooms fade. Many gardeners prize this late show, especially since hardy cyclamens thrive in shady spots and bring a touch of spring-like beauty to wooded areas.

Hardy cyclamen make an unusual groundcover under trees and shrubs. You'll enjoy both the leaves and the flowers.

Grow autumn crocus where you can enjoy the flowers but where their spring leaves won't smother delicate plants.

Bulbs for Indoor Bloom

There's nothing more heartwarming to a gardener than a pot of flowering bulbs on the windowsill in the depths of winter. Happily, it's relatively easy to convince most spring bulbs to rush the season a bit. The process is called "forcing," although there's not much force involved. You simply provide a condensed version of the winter the bulbs would otherwise get when growing in the ground outdoors.

Choosing Bulbs for Indoor Bloom

Most spring bulbs can be forced, but some perform better in pots than others. Spring-blooming crocus, Siberian squill (*Scilla sibirica*), glory-of-the-snow (*Chionodoxa luciliae*), and reticulated iris (*Iris reticulata*) are very easy to chill and bring into bloom. A few tulips that perform especially well in pots include pale orange 'Apricot Beauty', plum purple 'Atilla', and some of the small, rock garden species (such as the yellow-and-white *Tulipa tarda* and the yellow or bronze-pink *T. batalinii*).

Use hyacinth glasses to grow bulbs in water.

Daffodils are also gratifyingly easy to force. Although the large, yellow, trumpet daffodils are traditional favorites, many gardeners also enjoy smaller, free-flowering cultivars such as 'Pipit', 'Hawera', and 'Tete-a-tete'. Hyacinths, too, usually perform well in pots; a few that are especially good include pale pink 'Lady Derby', darker pink 'Pink Pearl', deep blue 'Blue Jacket', and salmon-pink 'Gypsy Queen'. Their sweet scent is ideal for curing a case of the winter blues!

For more ideas of bulbs to choose, check catalogs or garden-center bulb displays for the phrase "good for forcing." The individual plant entries in the "Guide

Extend the gardening season through the winter by growing a variety of bulbs for indoor bloom.

to Bulbs," starting on page 138, also call out those that are particularly well suited for forcing.

Preparing Bulbs for Forcing

The best time to plant bulbs for forcing is in late fall and early winter. Set the bulbs shoulder to shoulder in clay or plastic pots in ordinary, well-drained potting soil. The "nose" of the bulb should just peek above the soil surface. Label the pot with the name of the bulb and the date, water it thoroughly, and stash it in its winter quarters for chilling.

Giving Bulbs a Chance to Chill

Your bulbs need a cool, dark place while they're producing roots. The ideal temperatures for forcing bulbs are between 33° and 45°F (1° and 7°C). Some people use an unheated garage or basement; others set

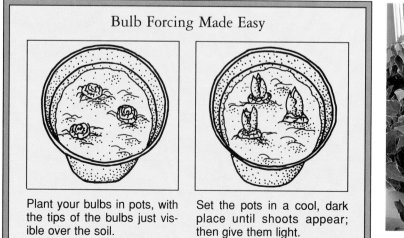

Bulb Forcing Made Easy

Plant your bulbs in pots, with the tips of the bulbs just visible over the soil.

Set the pots in a cool, dark place until shoots appear; then give them light.

If you plan to grow tulips indoors, look for those labeled "good for forcing."

To get a good show, you can plant many bulbs close together in the pot; it's okay if the bulbs touch.

'Paperwhite' narcissus are so easy to grow that they don't even need soil; try growing them in glass "pebbles."

their bulbs in a crawl space, potting shed, or cold frame. You may need to protect the bulbs with a heavy layer of straw, newspapers, or even old blankets to keep them from getting too cold.

Refrigerators can work well for chilling if you only have a few pots. They're especially useful if you live in a mild climate where outdoor winter temperatures don't get cold enough for proper chilling. An old-fashioned, round-top refrigerator (which does not have a frost-free feature) is the perfect place for storing potted bulbs. Modern refrigerators tend to be rather dry, so you should enclose potted bulbs in plastic bags (punch a few holes for air) to keep them from drying out too much.

If you don't have another place to chill your bulbs, you can try the mound technique. Simply set the bulb pots on the ground outdoors (perhaps in a corner of the vegetable garden), cover them with several inches of perlite or potting soil, and top the whole thing with a

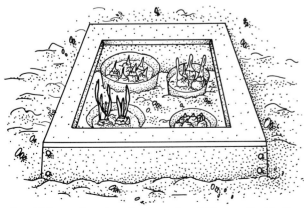

A cold frame is a handy place for chilling potted bulbs. You can also put them in a cool garage or a refrigerator.

thick insulating layer of straw or wood chips. Keep in mind, though, that this pile will provide an inviting home for local mice, which may move in and snack on your bulbs. It's also a messy job to dig your bulbs out of a snow-covered pile in the middle of winter.

Bringing Bulbs into Bloom

No matter where you chill your bulbs, check on them every few weeks to see if they need more water. At the same time, look for signs of growth. Your bulbs will signal they're ready to grow in two ways: Tiny white roots will be visible in the drainage holes of the pot, and new shoots will appear at the tops of the bulbs. Crocus and reticulated iris may be ready in as little as 8 weeks, while larger bulbs can take 12 weeks or more.

When the shoots are an inch or two (2.5 to 5 cm) tall, bring them inside to a cool, bright window. Fertilize lightly each time you water, and turn the pots regularly to keep the shoots from stretching unevenly toward the light. Keep pots away from radiators, hot-air registers, and other heat sources; bulbs like it cool.

Keep watering and fertilizing the bulbs until the foliage begins to wither. Transplant the bulbs to your garden at that time, or wait until fall. If you've cared for the bulbs well, they will likely settle in and bloom again in a few years.

Small bulbs, such as glory-of-the-snow, are ideal for growing under trees; they'll bloom and go dormant before the trees leaf out.

Bulbs also combine well with each other; try snowdrops with *Cyclamen coum*, for instance.

Bulbs and Companions

Whether you enjoy growing bulbs in formal displays or more natural-looking plantings, you can add extra interest by choosing compatible companion plants. Ideal companions will enhance the looks of the bulbs at bloom time and help to cover the ripening foliage later on.

Bulbs and Annuals

Showy bulbs such as tulips and hyacinths can make a dramatic feature when planted in rows or blocks. But it's even more exciting when you fill in between the bulbs with a pretty carpet of early-blooming annual flowers rather than leaving the soil bare or mulched. Good candidates for planting under bulbs include pansies, Johnny-jump-ups (*V. tricolor*), English daisies (*Bellis perennis*), and forget-me-nots (*Myosotis* spp.). As you choose companions, look for flower colors that complement those of your bulbs.

Summer-blooming annuals make great companions for bulbs in more informal plantings. As they grow, the annuals cover the bare soil and disguise the maturing bulb leaves. Self-sowing annuals are ideal for this purpose, since they will return year after year with little or no help for you. Good choices for sunny beds include California poppy (*Eschscholzia californica*), corn poppy (*Papaver rhoeas*), cornflower (*Centaurea cyanus*), and love-in-a-mist (*Nigella damascena*). You can also use annual transplants to fill in around bulbs, tucking them in before or just after the bulb blooms fade. Ageratum, dusty miller, and flowering tobacco (*Nicotiana alata*) are just a few good annuals to choose from. Within weeks, your annual transplants will fill the space left by the now-dormant bulbs.

Bulbs and Perennials

Tall bulbs, including lilies, ornamental onions (*Allium* spp.), and crown imperial (*Fritillaria imperalis*), usually look best near the middle or back of a bed or border. Planting them in between clumps of slightly shorter perennials makes attractive combinations, especially if the perennials bloom at the same time as the bulbs. For instance, Asiatic lilies are especially pretty with shasta daisies (*Chrysanthemum* x *superbum*), coral bells (*Heuchera sanguinea*), and Cupid's dart (*Catananche caerulea*) at their feet. You can also combine bulbs with taller perennials, such as delphiniums, mulleins (*Verbascum* spp.), and meadow rues (*Thalictrum* spp.), for a colorful background.

Bulbs and Groundcovers

Combining bulbs with groundcovers is a great way to go. The groundcover provides a pretty backdrop for the bulbs' flowers and then remains to add interest when the bulbs go dormant. Most bulbs have no trouble poking their flowers through a carpet of creeping stems and leaves. Many low-growing, spreading perennials, including thyme, sedums, creeping baby's-breath (*Gypsophila repens*), creeping veronicas (*Veronica* spp.), rock soapwort (*Saponaria ocymoides*), and sun rose (*Helianthemum nummularium*), can be used as groundcovers. In shady areas, try common periwinkle (*Vinca*

Combine Siberian squill and other early bulbs with spring-blooming shrubs and trees.

Mix bulbs with annuals and perennials to create beautiful color-theme plantings, such as this elegant white garden.

minor), creeping Jenny (*Lysimachia nummularia*), English ivy (*Hedera helix*), spotted lamium (*Lamium maculatum*), and self-heal (*Prunella* spp.).

Bulbs and Shrubs

Shrubs make wonderful companions for bulbs. You can create stunning garden scenes by grouping flowering shrubs and bulbs with similar bloom times and colors. Forsythia, for instance, creates a golden glow behind a mass of daffodils, while lilac beautifully echoes the colors of ornamental onions. The arching branches and fragrance of old-fashioned roses make them a classic companion for summer-blooming lilies. Viburnums (*Viburnum* spp.), mock oranges (*Philadelphus* spp.), hydrangeas (*Hydrangea* spp.), rhododendrons, and azaleas are some other wonderful flowering shrubs that look super with spring bulbs.

Evergreen shrubs, such as junipers, yews (*Taxus* spp.), and arborvitaes (*Thuja* spp.), complement flowering

bulbs throughout the year. Some evergreens have a gold, blue, or reddish cast to their foliage; keep this in mind as you combine them with bulbs. White or pink tulips, for instance, can create a soothing scene against the blue-gray cast of a juniper.

Bulbs and Trees

Bulbs and trees can also make colorful garden groupings. Spring bulbs are especially well suited for growing under deciduous trees, since they can get the sunlight they need before the leaves shade the ground. Spring-flowering bulbs that perform well under trees include crocus (*Crocus* spp.), squills (*Scilla sibirica* and *Puschkinia scilloides*), snowdrops (*Galanthus nivalis*), glory-of-the-snow (*Chionodoxa luciliae*), and daffodils. Summer-flowering bulbs that prefer some shade include tuberous begonias and caladiums (*Caladium* x *hortulanum*). For fall interest, add hardy cyclamen (*Cyclamen hederifolium*) and Italian arum (*Arum italicum*).

Make the most of your space by underplanting tall bulb flowers with low-growing plants, such as primroses.

Create seasonal displays by using tulips and other bulbs (along with colorful annuals) to accent shrubs and trees.

Bulbs for Cutting Gardens

The qualities that make bulbs great garden plants—their spectacular, long-lasting blooms and lovely scents—make them ideal cut flowers as well. But after you've put careful thought into combining your bulbs with other plants to create pretty garden scenes, the last thing you want to do is spoil the display by cutting the bulb flowers for indoor arrangements. The answer is to plant extra bulbs in a separate area—called a cutting garden—so you can pick all the flowers you want.

Starting a Cutting Garden

You can start planning your cutting garden any time of year, although summer is usually the best time; that will give you plenty of time to prepare the soil and place your bulb orders for fall planting.

Bulbs for cutting need the same conditions as those growing in ornamental gardens. A sunny area with fertile, well-drained soil suits most bulbs. If you have extra room in your vegetable garden, that's usually an ideal site to add a few blocks or rows of flowers for cutting. Otherwise, you'll need to remove the grass and weeds from your chosen site, dig the soil to loosen the top 8 to 10 inches (20 to 25 cm), and work in liberal amounts of organic matter to provide ideal rooting conditions.

Plant hardy bulbs in fall and tender ones in spring after the soil has warmed sufficiently. During the growing season, water as needed to keep the soil evenly moist. Mulch regularly to keep the roots cool, maintain steady soil moisture, and keep the flowers clean.

Snipping flowers from regular beds and borders is fine if you only do a few arrangements each season.

Stake tall plants, such as dahlias and gladioli, to keep the stems straight. For more details on soil preparation, planting, and maintenance, see "Growing Bulbs," starting on page 124.)

Gathering Cut Flowers

The best time to collect cut flowers is when the buds are just opening, not when they are in full bloom. If you are picking from bulbs that produce many flowers on a single stem, such as lilies or gladioli, cut them when the first few flowers at the bottom are opening.

When you cut the flowers, try to do it during a cool part of the day; morning is usually best. Take a bucket of lukewarm water and a sharp pair of clippers with you. Pick flowers with as few leaves as possible, so the bulbs can store enough energy for the next bloom season. As you

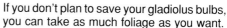

If you don't plan to save your gladiolus bulbs, you can take as much foliage as you want.

Growing bulbs in a cutting garden allows you to pick as many flowers as you want without spoiling your spring display.

The sap of daffodils may harm other flowers, so keep them in a separate container overnight before arranging them.

Small bulbs, such as grape hyacinths (*Muscari* spp.), can be charming for tiny bouquets and arrangements.

Cut tulips tend to bend toward a light source, so you may need to adjust your arrangements daily to keep them in line.

snip the stem from the rest of the plant, make a sloping, rather than straight, cut; this opens up a little more room for the stems to absorb water. Immediately plunge the cut flowers into the bucket, so they are in water up to the base of the flower. (If you are cutting dahlias, sear the bottom of the stem with the flame from a match before putting it in the water.)

Most professional florists "condition" their flowers by leaving them in a cool, dark place before arranging them. This conditioning can help flowers last a few days longer, but it isn't absolutely necessary if you want to arrange them right away. You can also buy commercial preservatives to help extend the life of your blooms, although the easiest method is simply to change the water every few days. Keeping the water clean will prevent the buildup of bacteria that can clog flower stems and shorten their life.

Dahlias make excellent cut flowers. Stake the plants of tall types to keep the stems growing straight.

Best Bulbs for Cutting

Cutting gardens are simple to plan and plant, since you don't need to worry about choosing compatible colors and heights. Listed below are some bulbs that make colorful, long-lasting cut flowers, arranged by bloom season; choose the ones you like best. For more information on any of these plants, see the "Guide to Bulbs," starting on page 138.

Spring Bloom
Ornamental onions (*Allium* spp.)
Hyacinth (*Hyacinthus orientalis*)
Summer snowflake (*Leucojum aestivum*)
Grape hyacinth (*Muscari armeniacum*)
Daffodils (*Narcissus* hybrids)
Tulips (*Tulipa* hybrids)

Summer Bloom
Canna (*Canna* x *generalis*)
Gladiolus (*Gladiolus* x *hortulanus*)
Asiatic lilies (*Lilium* Asiatic hybrids)
Trumpet lilies (*Lilium* Trumpet hybrids)

Fall Bloom
Dahlias (*Dahlia* hybrids)
Gladiolus (*Gladiolus* x *hortulanus*)
Oriental lilies (*Lilium* Oriental hybrids)
Magic lily (*Lycoris squamigera*)

GROWING BULBS

Planting bulbs for spring bloom requires some imagination on your part. After all, when you buy a six-pack of begonias, you can see just what you're getting. But when you buy bulbs, you get a bagful of promises: A bunch of brown-wrapped packets of plant energy that have the potential to transform themselves into colorful crocus or delightful daffodils. With proper planting and good care, your bulbs will be able to fulfill that potential, adding welcome color to your yard year after year. This chapter has all the information you need to grow strong, healthy bulbs and keep them vigorous for seasons to come.

As long as you give them the right growing conditions, newly bought bulbs are virtually guaranteed to bloom. "Buying Healthy Bulbs" on page 126 tells you how to pick the best-quality bulbs for surefire success. You'll find tips for selecting good bulbs at your local garden center, as well as guidelines for buying bulbs through mail-order sources.

Once you have your bulbs, you're ready to get them in the ground. "Planting Bulbs" on page 128 has the nitty-gritty on preparing your soil, as well as the basic techniques for planting in beds and borders. You'll also find tips for naturalizing bulbs in grassy areas to create easy-care, meadow-like areas.

After planting, most bulbs don't need a lot of fussing on your part to keep them going. "Caring for Bulbs" on page 130 covers all the basics of general bulb growing, from watering, fertilizing, and mulching to dealing with pest and disease problems. You even find tips for foiling animal pests.

Hardy bulbs, such as crocus and daffodils, are among the most low-maintenance plants, since they'll return year after year with minimal help from you. Tender bulbs—including gladiolus, dahlias, and cannas—are popular and showy, but they're also a bit more work in cold-winter areas because you'll need to dig them up every year and store them inside for the winter. "Handling Tender Bulbs" on page 134 explains your options for dealing with these temperature-sensitive beauties to enjoy their beautiful blooms year after year.

No matter what kinds of bulbs you grow, there's a good chance that you'll always want to grow more than you have. "Propagating Bulbs" on page 136 has all the secrets of expanding your bulb stock, from growing bulbs from seed to dividing existing plantings. With these simple techniques, you'll find out how easy it is to expand your plantings without shrinking your bank account.

Start with healthy bulbs and plant them in the right conditions, and they'll reward you with years of beautiful blooms. Many kinds, including reticulated iris (*Iris reticulata*), will spread to form large, showy clumps.

Lily bulbs may have fleshy roots when you buy them; other bulbs shouldn't have roots.

Buy generous quantities of bulbs and plant them in drifts or large clumps to create a dramatic spring display in the garden.

Buying Healthy Bulbs

A key part of growing bulbs successfully is starting with healthy plants. By being a smart shopper, you can get the best bulbs for your garden at the best possible price.

Knowing What to Look For

With bulbs, as with most things, you get what you pay for. High-quality, full-sized bulbs command top dollar, based on the amount of time and labor it takes to produce them, but you can rely on them for spectacular results.

A higher price, however, doesn't always mean that one tulip or daffodil cultivar is better than another. New cultivars tend to be much more expensive than older ones that have been around awhile. New cultivars are fun to try, but the old standbys that have proven to be good performers through the years are usually both economical and dependable.

A top-quality bulb is firm to the touch (not mushy or squishy) and free of large blemishes or scars. Some bulbs, such as tulips and hyacinths, may have a trace of blue mold on them. A few small mold spots will not harm the bulb, but a noticeable layer may indicate that the bulb was stored improperly before being offered for sale.

Look for bulbs that show little or no root or shoot growth except for a pale growth bud at the top. (Lilies are an exception, since they often have fleshy roots attached.) It's wise to shop early in the season so you can get the bulbs before they dry out from sitting in a store for weeks.

Investing in good-quality bulbs will help ensure great results in the garden year after year.

Bulbs come in an array of shapes and sizes. Buy those that are plump and firm; avoid shriveled or discolored bulbs.

To get the best possible performance from hybrid tulips, remove the old bulbs and replant new ones each fall.

Handling Bulbs When You Get Them Home

You've shopped carefully to get the best bulbs. Now follow through and handle them properly when you get them home. In most cases, it's best to plant the bulbs within a few days so they'll have plenty of time to adapt to their new home and send out a good crop of roots.

If you can't plant right away, store your bulbs in a cool, dark, and relatively dry place until you're ready for them. Keep them in the paper or mesh bags they came in. A refrigerator can be handy for storing spring bulbs but is too cold for summer bulbs, such as gladioli or dahlias. Keep summer bulbs in a moderately cool spot—such as a cupboard or closet in a basement, attached garage, or utility room—until you're ready to start them indoors or plant them outdoors after your last spring frost date.

If you can find them, buy hardy cyclamen as plants rather than as tubers; plants tend to establish more quickly.

Older, established cultivars of tulips tend to be reasonably priced and are generally dependable bloomers.

To get a good show of bloom from the first year on, plant your bulbs in clumps rather than as individuals.

It's easy to plant in a prepared bed: Just dig a hole, set in the bulbs, and cover them with the soil you removed.

Planting Bulbs

The great thing about most bulbs is that they can adapt to a wide range of growing conditions. But if you really want your bulbs to thrive, it's worth putting some thought into giving them the best conditions possible. Take a little time to prepare a good growing site and plant your bulbs properly. Then you can stand back and enjoy the bounty of beautiful flowers in the years to come.

Getting the Soil Ready

Many bulbs can grow for years in the same place, so it's worth putting some effort into preparing an ideal planting site. How much work that will take depends on what kind of soil you have.

In "Soil and Site Conditions" on page 23, you learned how to tell whether your soil is loamy, clayey, or sandy. Bulbs tend to thrive in soil that's on the loamy or sandy side, since good drainage is critical for most bulbs. Very sandy soil, however, can be too dry and infertile. Clayey soil holds a good amount of nutrients, but it can also hold too much water. Loamy soil tends to hold an adequate supply of nutrients and moisture without getting waterlogged.

If your soil isn't naturally loamy, you can improve its drainage and fertility by adding some organic matter before you plant your bulbs. Spread a 1- to 3-inch (2.5 to 7.5 cm) layer of compost or chopped leaves over the planting area, then work it into the top 10 to 12 inches (25 to 30 cm) of soil. (When you're only planting small bulbs, such as crocus and grape hyacinths, you can get away with loosening just the top 4 to 6 inches [10 to 15 cm] of soil.) Or, if you're digging individual holes, work a handful of organic matter into the soil at the base of each hole, and add another handful to the soil you use to refill the hole. As it breaks down, the organic matter will release a small but steady supply of nutrients for good bulb growth.

Planting Bulbs in Beds and Borders

Once you've loosened the soil, planting is easy—just dig the hole to the proper depth, pop in the bulb, and cover it with soil. The proper depth will vary, depending on what bulbs you're growing. A general rule of thumb is that the base of a bulb or corm should be three to four

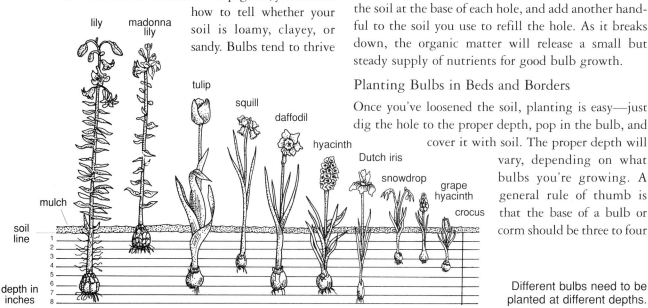

Different bulbs need to be planted at different depths.

If you're just planting a few bulbs, you could use a bulb planter or a trowel to make individual holes.

When you're planting in masses, it's usually easiest to dig a large planting area that can hold many bulbs at once.

times the height of the bulb. For example, a crocus corm that measures 1 inch (2.5 cm) high should be planted 3 to 4 inches (7.5 to 10 cm) deep; a 2-inch (5 cm) high tulip bulb needs a hole 6 to 8 inches (15 to 20 cm) deep. If your soil is on the sandy side, plant a bit deeper. To find out the best planting depth for your bulbs, check the catalog description or package label or refer to the individual entries in the "Guide to Bulbs," starting on page 138.

Set the bulb in the hole with the pointed growth bud facing upward. If you can't tell which side should be up—as often happens with small bulbs such as Grecian windflowers (*Anemone blanda*)—set the bulb on its side or just drop it in the hole and hope for the best. Most bulbs have a strong will to grow, and they'll find a way to send up their shoots.

Space the bulbs so each has ample room to grow. As a general rule, you should leave 5 to 6 inches (12.5 to 15 cm) between large bulbs and 1 to 3 inches (2.5 to 7.5 cm) between small bulbs. Once you've got the spacing the way you want it, carefully replace the soil around the bulbs to refill the hole. Firm the soil by patting it with your hand or the back of a rake, then water thoroughly.

Planting Bulbs in Grassy Areas

When you choose to "naturalize" bulbs in a lawn or meadow, you don't have the luxury of preparing a nice, loose planting area all at once. Fortunately, the bulbs that grow well in these situations are pretty tough. (For advice on choosing the best bulbs, see "Best Bulbs for Naturalizing" on page 121.)

The easiest bulbs to plant are the small ones, such as crocus and Siberian squill (*Scilla sibirica*). Simply get down on your hands and knees with a narrow trowel, dandelion digger, or garden knife. Insert the tool into the soil to lift up a flap of turf, or wiggle the tool back and forth to make a small hole. Insert the bulb, firm the soil and sod over it, and water thoroughly.

For larger bulbs, it's often easier to use a shovel or spade to remove a larger patch of turf, about 1 foot (30 cm) square. Loosen the soil to the proper depth, plant the bulbs, replace the turf, and water. You can also buy special bulb planting tools to make individual holes for your large bulbs. Hand-held planters look like deep cookie cutters and work pretty much the same way. They are fairly inexpensive but can be really tiring to use. A similar type of planter that's mounted on a handle is a little easier to use, since you can push the cutting edge into the ground with your foot instead of your hand.

For even easier planting, try an auger attachment that connects to a regular hand-held power drill. These tools can be hard to use around rocks and tree roots, but they let you make many holes quickly under most conditions.

For best growth from hyacinths and other spring bulbs, make sure the soil is evenly moist in fall and spring; summer moisture is less critical.

To grow tall bulbs without staking, site them in a spot that's sheltered from wind.

Caring for Bulbs

Hardy bulbs—including daffodils, crocus, and other dependable favorites—are about as close to "no work" as you can get. You just plant them once, and they come back year after year. Many will even multiply over time to produce large sweeps of blooms.

But as with any other garden plants, a little extra care from you can help your bulbs grow and look better. In this section, you'll find tips for keeping your bulbs in the best condition possible, with good gardening practices such as watering, mulching, fertilizing, staking, deadheading, and controlling pests and diseases.

Watering for Good Growth

Watering is most important when your bulbs are actively growing. This means fall and spring for fall- or spring-blooming bulbs and spring through summer for summer-blooming bulbs. During these times, most bulbs can survive a moderate drought without watering, but they may not bloom well the following year.

To get your bulbs off to a good start, water them thoroughly at planting time. If there's a dry spell when your bulbs are growing, water them as you would your other garden plants to keep them vigorous. For more information on knowing when and how to water, see "Watering" on page 53.

Mulching

Mulching your bulbs is one of the best ways to keep them healthy. Mulch will help to hold moisture in the soil and minimize rapid temperature changes, providing ideal rooting conditions. It shades the soil and helps to keep bulbs cool, protecting the shoots of bulbs from being lured out of the ground too early in spring. Mulch also benefits summer-flowering bulbs, such as lilies, which dislike hot, dry soil. Mulch discourages weeds from sprouting and prevents rain from splashing soil onto bulb leaves and flowers, keeping your bulb plants clean and discouraging disease problems.

There is no one ideal mulch. When you shop for mulches, choose the kind that looks best to you and that you can afford. Depending on where you live, you may be able to find locally available materials—such as cocoa bean shells or pine needles—at good prices. Wood chips or shredded bark are available in most parts of the country. (Look for small chips, not big bark nuggets.) A mulch of pea-sized gravel can work well, too. Homemade or purchased compost can make a good mulch, either alone or as a layer under another mulch. A "living mulch" of low-growing annuals or perennials may be the best of all, since it serves the

Mulches keep weeds down, help to maintain soil moisture, and prevent soil from splashing onto the flowers.

purpose of a regular mulch and provides flowers as well.

Mulch your bulbs after planting in fall or spring. Apply a 1- to 2-inch (2.5 to 5 cm) layer of mulch over the soil. Avoid putting on too much, or your bulbs may have trouble poking their shoots up through the mulch. To protect hardy bulbs (such as daffodils and crocus), add more mulch each fall to keep it at the right depth.

Fertilizing

Most bulbs will get along just fine without a lot of extra fertilizer. Working compost or other organic matter into the soil at planting time and using it as a mulch will provide much of the nutrient supply your bulbs need.

For top-notch growth, you can also sprinkle commercial organic fertilizer over the soil, following the package directions. Use a mix blended especially for bulbs, if you can find one; otherwise, a general garden fertilizer is acceptable. Fertilize both spring-blooming and fall-flowering bulbs in spring. Summer-flowering bulbs usually grow best with several small applications of fertilizer in early- to mid-summer.

Tuberous begonias, lilies, and other bulbs growing in pots benefit from weekly or bimonthly doses of liquid fertilizer. Spray the leaves or water the plants with diluted fish emulsion or compost tea (made by soaking a shovelful of finished compost in a bucket of water for about a week, then straining out the soaked compost).

Staking

The easiest approach to staking plants is to reduce the need for it. Whenever possible, site your bulbs on the

Spring is a good time to fertilize spring- and fall-blooming bulbs; you may also add bonemeal in fall.

Minimizing Mulch Problems

While mulch has many good points in its favor, there are a few disadvantages. If your soil tends to be on the clayey side, mulch may hold in too much moisture, promoting bulb rot. Mulch can also provide an ideal hiding place for slugs and snails.

If you notice any of these problems, wait until the soil has dried out some in early summer before applying a summer mulch. Over winter, use a light mulch such as evergreen boughs to protect emerging bulb shoots without holding in extra moisture.

sheltered side of hedges, fences, or screens, so the plants will be protected from the wind. Also look for compact cultivars of your favorite flowers; shorter stems are less prone to damage.

Of course, there are also times when you don't want all of your bulbs to stand stiff and upright. Perhaps you enjoy a more casual look, where the bulbs are allowed to lean against and mingle with other plants. If you aren't sure which of your bulbs would benefit from staking, watch them for a year or two and see which look like they could use some help.

If you mulch your bulbs, use a layer no more than 2 inches (5 cm) thick; otherwise, it may smother the shoots.

Most bulb seedpods aren't especially showy, but those of ornamental onions (*Allium* spp.) can be quite decorative.

When you want the biggest possible dahlia flowers, remove the side buds to leave one main bud on each shoot.

There are two tricks to staking bulbs properly—choosing natural-looking stakes and putting them in early. Don't wait until a stem is full grown and leaning like the Leaning Tower of Pisa to insert a stake. The results are rarely satisfactory for you or the plant.

Manufacturers sell various metal and wooden stakes, rings, and hoops to support plants. Materials painted green or brown tend to be the least noticeable. Some gardeners use twiggy tree or shrub prunings for plant supports. These brushy stakes are plentiful and free, and they are nearly invisible in the garden when the plants grow up through them.

Select supports that are about three-quarters of the plant's ultimate height. (Allow another 6 inches [15 cm] for the part of the stake that will be underground.) Top-heavy plants such as lilies need stakes that are about the same height as the mature height of the plant.

Whatever kind of stake you choose, put it in the ground as soon as the bulb shoots are visible. Place the stake behind the plant (as you will view it from the front of the bed or border) so the support is less visible. Insert each stake a few inches away from the shoot to avoid stabbing the bulb. Push the stake at least 6 inches (15 cm) into the soil to steady it.

As the bulb shoot grows, attach it to the stake with a flexible tie, such as green or brown yarn or string. Tie a knot to the stake, loop the yarn or string around the stem, and then tie it back to the stake. Never choke a stem by tying a knot directly around it. Start tying near the base of the stem; add another tie every 6 to 8 inches (15 to 20 cm) as the stem grows.

Deadheading

To gardeners, deadheading means removing faded flowers and developing seedpods from plants. Whether or not you decide to deadhead your

Wait until bulbs' leaves turn yellow to remove them.

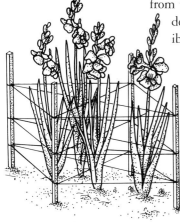

Stake-and-string cages can be useful for gladioli.

Removing spent flowers and developing seedpods can help keep bulb plantings looking good longer.

bulbs is really a matter of personal choice. Some gardeners routinely deadhead large bulbs, such as daffodils, hyacinths, and tulips. They claim that this prevents the bulbs from expending energy on seed production, directing all their energy to ripening their leaves and replenishing their food reserves. However, many species tulips and daffodils grow just fine year after year if allowed to set seed; in fact, they may even reseed and produce more bulbs. Small bulbs (such as crocus and grape hyacinths) will also spread by reseeding to form large sweeps of bloom.

If you do choose to deadhead your bulbs, pinch off the developing seedpod with your fingernails, or cut it off with clippers. For a neater appearance, you can instead cut the seedpod and the stem beneath it down to the top stem leaves (if there are any) or to the ground. On lilies, remove only the top part of the stem that holds the seedpods; don't cut off any leaves.

Controlling Pests and Diseases

Most bulbs suffer from few pests and diseases. Those pests and diseases that do attack are usually the same as those you find on your other garden plants. Some of the most common problems include aphids, whiteflies, Japanese beetles, spider mites, slugs and snails, thrips, cutworms, Botrytis blight, and powdery mildew. For more information on identifying and controlling these and other problems, see "Pests and Problems of Annuals" on page 57.

Deer, rabbits, mice, and other animal pests can also plague bulb gardeners. You can try to discourage pests by planting daffodil bulbs, which are poisonous and usually avoided by animals. Some say that the strong

Prevent powdery mildew on tuberous begonias by giving them a site with good air circulation. Pinch off affected leaves.

odor of crown imperial (*Fritillaria imperialis*) bulbs and plants repels voles, mice, and squirrels. Pet dogs and cats can be useful for discouraging local wildlife, but they may cause damage, too.

It is possible to take preventive measures when planting where mice, voles, shrews, and squirrels are especially troublesome. Although it takes some doing, you can fashion bulb crates—sort of like lobster traps—out of sturdy wire mesh. Choose mesh with a grid size of about 1 inch (2.5 cm). Small animals can sneak through larger mesh, while your bulb shoots may not be able to poke through smaller mesh. Dig a hole large enough to hold the crate, so the top is just below the soil surface. Place the crate in the hole and backfill with some of the soil you removed. Plant your bulbs in the crate, then fill the rest of the cage with soil and close the lid. Use the remaining soil to cover the lid and fill in around the rest of the cage.

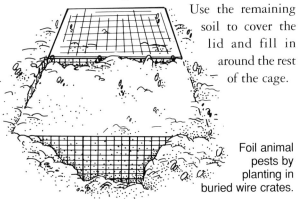

Foil animal pests by planting in buried wire crates.

Whiteflies are common on greenhouse plants but can also feed on garden plants. Control with insecticidal soap spray.

Canna x *generalis*   Cannaceae

CANNA

Cannas are drought-tolerant, but they grow even better with mulch and watering during dry spells. Pinch off spent flowers to prolong bloom.

DESCRIPTION: Cannas grow from thick rhizomes. They produce tall, sturdy stems with large, oval, green or reddish purple leaves from spring until frost. The stems are topped with showy clusters of broad-petaled flowers up to 5 inches (12.5 cm) across from mid- through late-summer. The flowers bloom in shades of pink, red, orange, and yellow, as well as bicolors.

HEIGHT AND SPREAD: Height 2–6 feet (60–180 cm) or more; spread 12–24 inches (30–60 cm).

BEST SITE AND CLIMATE: Full sun to partial shade; average to moist, well-drained soil with added organic matter. Usually hardy in Zones 7–10; elsewhere, grown as annuals or stored indoors in winter.

GROWING GUIDELINES: For the earliest show, start rhizomes indoors in pots about 1 month before your last frost date. Set out started plants 2–3 weeks after the last frost date. Or plant rhizomes directly into the garden around that time, setting them 3–4 inches (7.5–10 cm) deep and 12–18 inches (30–45 cm) apart. North of Zone 7 (and in Zone 7, if you want to ensure survival), dig the rhizomes before or just after the first frost and store them indoors for winter. In warm areas, divide the rhizomes every 3–4 years in spring.

LANDSCAPE USES: Grow them alone in masses, or plant them with annuals and perennials in beds and borders. Cannas also grow well in containers.

Colchicum speciosum   Liliaceae

SHOWY AUTUMN CROCUS

Showy autumn crocus grows from large, plump corms. Once established, each corm will produce showy clumps of rosy pink flowers in late summer to early fall.

DESCRIPTION: Wide, flat, glossy green leaves emerge in late fall or early spring, elongate through spring, then turn yellow and die to the ground in early summer. Rosy pink, 4-inch (10 cm) wide, goblet-shaped, stemless flowers rise directly from the ground in late summer to early fall.

HEIGHT AND SPREAD: Height of leaves to about 8 inches (20 cm); flowers 4–6 inches (10–15 cm) tall. Spread to about 6 inches (15 cm).

BEST SITE AND CLIMATE: Full sun to partial shade; average, well-drained soil. Zones 4–9.

GROWING GUIDELINES: Plant corms in mid- to late-summer, as soon as they are available; they may begin to bloom even before you plant them if you delay. Set the corms in individual holes or in larger planting areas dug about 4 inches (10 cm) deep. Space bulbs 6 inches (15 cm) apart. Divide just after the leaves die down only if needed for propagation.

LANDSCAPE USES: Showy autumn crocus is beautiful but a little tricky to site effectively. It's usually best coming up through low groundcovers or under shrubs, where the coarse spring leaves won't detract from or smother other flowers.

OTHER SPECIES:

C. speciosum produces rosy pink, fall flowers with white centers. 'Waterlily' has large, double flowers. 'Album' has white flowers. Zones 4–9.

Crocus speciosus Iridaceae

SHOWY CROCUS

If you grow showy crocus in lawn areas, wait until the leaves turn yellow to start mowing in summer, and stop mowing in early fall—as soon as the first flower buds appear.

DESCRIPTION: Showy crocus grows from a small corm. Thin, green, grass-like leaves with a white center stripe rise in spring, grow, and go dormant by midsummer. The stemless flowers emerge from the soil in early- to mid-fall. The goblet-shaped, 1–2-inch (2.5–5 cm) wide blooms are usually lavender purple with violet purple veins.

HEIGHT AND SPREAD: Height of leaves to 6 inches (15 cm); flowers usually grow 4–6 inches (10–15 cm) tall. Spread to about 2 inches (5 cm).

BEST SITE AND CLIMATE: Full sun; average, well-drained soil. Zones 5–9.

GROWING GUIDELINES: Plant in late summer, as soon as they are available. Set them in individual holes or larger planting areas dug about 3 inches (7.5 cm) deep. Space the corms 4–6 inches (10–15 cm) apart. Established clumps of showy crocus will spread and reseed to cover large areas. Divide clumps in midsummer if needed for propagation.

LANDSCAPE USES: Looks charming popping out of low groundcovers, such as English ivy (*Hedera helix*) or common periwinkle (*Vinca minor*). It's also excellent for naturalizing in low-maintenance areas.

OTHER SPECIES:

C. sativus, saffron crocus, has purple flowers with deep purple veins. The showy orange-red stigmas are dried and used as a dye and a flavoring for food. The corms prefer dry soil in summer. Zones 6–9.

Crocus vernus Iridaceae

DUTCH CROCUS

Dutch crocus are a welcome sight after a long, cold winter. After bloom, the leaves continue to elongate until they ripen and die back to the ground in early summer.

DESCRIPTION: Dutch crocus grow from small corms. They appear in late winter to early spring, with leaves and flowers at the same time. The grass-like leaves are thin and green with a white center stripe. Goblet-shaped, stemless flowers up to 3 inches (7.5 cm) across bloom just above the leaves. The flowers are white, lavender, purple, or yellow; they may be striped with contrasting colors.

HEIGHT AND SPREAD: Height of leaves to 8 inches (20 cm); flowers usually to 4 inches (10 cm) tall. Spread 1–3 inches (2.5–7.5 cm).

BEST SITE AND CLIMATE: Full sun to partial shade (under deciduous trees and shrubs); average, well-drained soil. Zones 3–8.

GROWING GUIDELINES: Plant the corms in fall. Set them pointed side up in individual holes or larger planting areas dug 2–4 inches (5–10 cm) deep. Space the corms 2 inches (5 cm) apart. Dutch crocus usually return year after year and spread to form showy clumps. Interplanting crocus corms with daffodil bulbs (which are toxic if eaten) may help discourage damage from mice.

LANDSCAPE USES: Include them in beds and borders for early color. Grow them in containers for outdoor spring bloom or winter forcing indoors. They are excellent for naturalizing in lawn areas if you can wait until late spring (when the crocus leaves have turned yellow) before you start mowing.

Cyclamen hederifolium   Primulaceae
HARDY CYCLAMEN

Hardy cyclamen grow well under shrubs and trees—even in dry summer shade—and are attractive through most of the year. Top-dress with a thin layer of compost in late summer.

DESCRIPTION: Hardy cyclamen grow from smooth tubers. They bloom in early fall, with leafless flower stalks topped with pink or white flowers. The 1-inch (2.5 cm) long, nodding flowers have upward-pointing petals. Handsome, heart-shaped, silver-marked, green leaves emerge shortly after the blooms finish. The leaves die back by midsummer but return again by midfall.

HEIGHT AND SPREAD: Height and spread of flowers and foliage 4–6 inches (10–15 cm).

BEST SITE AND CLIMATE: Partial shade; average, well-drained soil. Zones 5–9.

GROWING GUIDELINES: Many commercial cyclamen sources sell wild-collected tubers. Avoid supporting this irresponsible practice: Buy nursery-propagated tubers or start your own from seed. Soak the seed overnight, then sow it ¼ inch (6 mm) deep in a pot. Enclose the pot in a plastic bag, then set it in a dark place. Check every month for signs of sprouting; this may take from a few weeks to a few years. Set plants into the garden in spring or summer. Or plant dormant tubers shallowly in summer, making sure the smooth, unmarked side is on the bottom. The top of the tuber should be about 1 inch (2.5 cm) below the soil surface. Space hardy cyclamen 6 inches (15 cm) apart.

LANDSCAPE USES: Hardy cyclamen look good in shady spots with ferns and hellebores (*Helleborus* spp.).

Dahlia hybrids   Compositae
DAHLIAS

Pinch off stem tips in early summer to promote bushy growth and more (but smaller) flowers. Or, to get the largest flowers, pinch off sideshoots to leave one or two main stems.

DESCRIPTION: Dahlias grow from long, slender, tuberous roots. Some types, known as bedding dahlias, form compact, bushy plants; others produce the tall, large-flowered border favorites. Both types have upright stems with divided, green (or sometimes purple-tinted) leaves. Dahlias bloom from midsummer through fall, with flowers 1–8 inches (2.5–20 cm) across or more. They come in almost every color but true blue—even in near black and bicolors. The flowers are available in many different forms, including spiky-petaled cactus types, daisy-like singles, puffy-centered anemone types, and globe-shaped ball and pompon types.

HEIGHT AND SPREAD: Height varies from 1 foot (30 cm) for bedding types to 5 feet (1.5 m) for border types. Spread to 1 foot (30 cm) for bedding types and 4 feet (1.2 m) for border types.

BEST SITE AND CLIMATE: Full sun; average, well-drained soil. Hardy in Zones 9 and 10; elsewhere, grown as annuals or stored indoors for winter.

GROWING GUIDELINES: Start bedding types from seed sown indoors 6–8 weeks before your last frost date. Plant seed ⅛ inch (3 mm) deep. Set plants out in the garden 1–2 weeks after the last frost date; space them 10–12 inches (25–30 cm) apart.

In Northern areas, start tuberous roots indoors in large pots 2–3 weeks before your last frost date; set started plants out 1–2 weeks after the last frost

CROWN IMPERIAL

Thousands of dahlia cultivars are available through garden centers and mail-order catalogs. Check pictures and descriptions to find the colors and flower forms you like best.

Crown imperials may take a few seasons to get established and bloom well; mature clumps can live for many years. All parts of the plant have a musky (some say skunk-like) odor.

date. Elsewhere, plant the roots directly into the garden around the last frost date. Dig a hole about 6 inches (15 cm) deep and set in the roots, so the purplish eyes are 2–4 inches (5–10 cm) below the soil surface. When planting tall border dahlias, also insert a stake at planting time to avoid damaging the roots later on.

Mulch in summer and water during dry spells. Cut or pinch off spent flowers regularly to prolong the bloom season.

Border dahlias can stay in the ground all winter in areas that are generally frost-free. With a thick layer of mulch, they often overwinter in Zone 8 gardens as well (although you may want to dig up your favorites in fall for indoor storage). In Zones 7 and north, treat dahlias as annuals (buy new roots or start new plants from seed each spring). Or dig up the roots in fall, before or just after the first frost, and store them indoors in a cool but frost-free area. Before replanting in spring, divide the root clumps in half or thirds, making sure each section has some of the stem attached.

LANDSCAPE USES: Bedding dahlias add cheerful color to the fronts of beds and borders, as well as to pots and window boxes. Tall-growing types are excellent for late-summer and fall interest in the middle and back of beds and borders. Include some in the cutting garden, too—they last well in arrangements.

DESCRIPTION: Crown imperial grows from a large, fleshy bulb. Sturdy shoots of green stems and glossy green leaves emerge in early spring and elongate for several weeks. By mid- to late-spring, the tall stems are topped with a tuft of green leaves and hanging, bell-shaped, yellow, orange, or red flowers about 2 inches (5 cm) long. Soon after bloom, the leaves and stems turn yellow; they die back to the ground by midsummer.

HEIGHT AND SPREAD: Height 24–48 inches (60–120 cm); spread to 12 inches (30 cm).

BEST SITE AND CLIMATE: Full spring sun; average to sandy, well-drained soil. Zones 5–9.

GROWING GUIDELINES: Plant the bulbs in late summer or early fall, as soon as they are available. Dig a large hole for each bulb or prepare a large planting area; make either about 8 inches (20 cm) deep. Loosen the soil at the base of the hole to promote good drainage. When you set the bulb in the hole, tilt it slightly to one side to discourage water from collecting in the depression at the top of the bulb. Space bulbs 12 inches (30 cm) apart. Lift and divide bulbs in summer only if needed for propagation.

LANDSCAPE USES: They make striking spring accents for beds and borders. Good companions include honesty (*Lunaria annua*), forget-me-nots (*Myosotis* spp.), and daffodils. Follow them with later-blooming annuals.

Fritillaria meleagris   Liliaceae

CHECKERED LILY

The nodding flowers of checkered lilies add a charming touch to spring gardens. Naturalize them in wild areas, or plant them in clumps in beds and borders.

OTHER COMMON NAMES: Guinea-hen flower, snake's-head lily.

DESCRIPTION: Checkered lily grows from small bulbs. Slender, arching stems with narrow, gray-green leaves rise in early spring. By midspring, broad, nodding, bell-like blooms dangle from the ends of the nodding stems. The 1–2-inch (2.5–5 cm) long flowers range in color from white to deep purple; many are marked with a checkered pattern. Checkered lilies die back to the ground by midsummer.

HEIGHT AND SPREAD: Height to 12 inches (30 cm); spread 2–4 inches (5–10 cm).

BEST SITE AND CLIMATE: Partial shade; average, well-drained soil. Zones 3–8.

GROWING GUIDELINES: Plant in early fall, as soon as the bulbs are available. Dig the holes or planting areas 2–3 inches (5–7.5 cm) deep. Space bulbs 4–6 inches (10–15 cm) apart. Leave established clumps undisturbed to form large sweeps of spring color.

LANDSCAPE USES: Checkered lilies look lovely when naturalized in masses in woodland or meadow gardens. Or grow them in beds and borders under deciduous trees; these small bulbs combine beautifully with ferns and hellebores (*Helleborus* spp.).

CULTIVARS: 'Alba' has white flowers.

Galanthus nivalis   Amaryllidaceae

COMMON SNOWDROP

Common snowdrops are among the earliest flowers to bloom in the spring garden. Established bulbs are trouble-free; they will spread and reseed freely.

DESCRIPTION: Common snowdrops grow from small bulbs. Each bulb produces two or three flat, narrow, green leaves and an upright to arching green flower stem in midwinter through early spring. Dainty, nodding flowers to 1 inch (2.5 cm) long bloom at the tips of the stems in late winter or early spring. The single or double flowers are white; each of the shorter, inner petals has a green tip. Plants die back to the ground by early summer.

HEIGHT AND SPREAD: Height of flowers and foliage to 6 inches (15 cm); spread 2–3 inches (5–7.5 cm).

BEST SITE AND CLIMATE: Full sun to partial shade; average to moist, well-drained soil with added organic matter. Zones 3–9.

GROWING GUIDELINES: Plant bulbs in fall. Set them in individual holes or larger planting areas dug 3–4 inches (7.5–10 cm) deep. Space bulbs 3–4 inches (7.5–10 cm) apart.

LANDSCAPE USES: Grow clumps of common snowdrop in the garden with other early flowers, such as snow crocus and Christmas rose (*Helleborus niger*). Or naturalize them in lawns, groundcovers, and low-maintenance areas or under deciduous trees and shrubs. (If you grow them in lawns, you'll have to wait until the leaves have turned yellow or brown to mow.)

CULTIVARS: 'Flore Pleno' has double flowers.

| *Gladiolus* x *hortulanus* | Iridaceae | *Hyacinthoides hispanica* | Liliaceae |

GLADIOLUS

SPANISH BLUEBELLS

Gladioli bloom in nearly every color but true blue; many have spots or splashes of contrasting colors. For cut flowers, pick them just as the bottom bud begins to open.

Established patches of Spanish bluebells increase quickly, often to the point of becoming invasive. Removing spent flower stalks will minimize reseeding; mow unwanted plants.

DESCRIPTION: Gladioli grow from flattened corms. They produce tall fans of flat, sword-shaped, green leaves. A slender flower stem rises from the center of each fan in summer to early fall (depending on the planting time). The flower stem is topped with a many-budded spike that blooms from the bottom up. The buds produce open, funnel-shaped flowers up to 4 inches (10 cm) across. The leaves usually turn yellow several weeks after bloom.

HEIGHT AND SPREAD: Height 2–5 feet (60–150 cm); spread 6–12 inches (15–30 cm).

BEST SITE AND CLIMATE: Full sun; average, well-drained soil. Usually hardy in Zones 8–10; elsewhere, grown as annuals or stored indoors for winter.

GROWING GUIDELINES: Start planting the corms outdoors after the last frost date in spring. Set them in individual holes or larger planting areas dug 4–6 inches (10–25 cm) deep. Space the corms 4–6 inches (10–25 cm) apart. To extend the bloom season, plant more corms every 2 weeks until midsummer. Tall-flowering types benefit from staking. In Zone 7 and colder areas, dig the corms before or just after the first frost, and store them indoors in a frost-free area.

LANDSCAPE USES: The spiky blooms add excitement to the middle and back of beds and borders. They are also a must for the cutting garden.

DESCRIPTION: Spanish bluebells grow from small bulbs. In spring, the plants form clumps of sprawling, strap-shaped, green leaves. Upright, leafless flower stems topped with spikes of many bell-shaped blooms appear in late spring. The ¾-inch (18 mm) wide flowers bloom in white, pink, or shades of purple-blue. Plants go dormant by midsummer. Spanish bluebells are still sold under a variety of former names, including *Scilla campanulata, Scilla hispanica,* and *Endymion hispanicus.*

HEIGHT AND SPREAD: Height of flowers 12–18 inches (30–45 cm); leaves usually to 8 inches (20 cm) tall. Spread 4–6 inches (10–15 cm).

BEST SITE AND CLIMATE: Full sun to partial shade; average, well-drained soil with added organic matter. Zones 4–8.

GROWING GUIDELINES: Plant the bulbs in fall. Set them in individual holes or larger planting areas dug 3–4 inches (7.5–10 cm) deep. Space bulbs 4–6 inches (10–25 cm) apart.

LANDSCAPE USES: Include clumps in beds and borders, combine them with groundcovers, or naturalize them in woodlands and low-maintenance areas.

OTHER SPECIES:

H. non-scripta, English bluebells, has violet-blue flowers on arching, 12-inch (30 cm) tall stems. It is sometimes listed in catalogs as *Scilla non-scripta, S. nutans,* or *Endymion non-scriptus.* Zones 5–8.

| *Hyacinthus orientalis* | Liliaceae | *Iris reticulata* | Iridaceae |

HYACINTH

After the first year, hyacinth bloom spikes tend to be smaller; in some cases, they may not flower at all. Plant new bulbs every year or two to ensure a good display.

DESCRIPTION: Hyacinths grow from plump bulbs. Sturdy shoots with wide, strap-shaped, green leaves and upright flower stalks emerge in early spring. By midspring, each stalk is topped with a dense spike of starry, 1-inch (2.5 cm) wide, powerfully fragrant flowers. The single or double flowers bloom in a wide range of colors, including white, pink, red, orange, yellow, blue, and purple. Hyacinths go dormant in early summer.

HEIGHT AND SPREAD: Height 8–12 inches (20–30 cm); spread to 4 inches (15 cm).

BEST SITE AND CLIMATE: Full sun; average, well-drained soil with added organic matter. Zones 4–8.

GROWING GUIDELINES: Plant bulbs in midfall. Set them in individual holes or larger planting areas dug 5–6 inches (12.5–15 cm) deep. Space the bulbs 6–10 inches (15–20 cm) apart. Double-flowered types may need staking. Remove spent flower stalks. For propagation, dig up and divide crowded clumps as the leaves yellow.

LANDSCAPE USES: Hyacinths contribute cheerful spring color to flower beds and borders. Combine them with primroses and pansies for extra excitement. They also grow well in containers for spring bloom outdoors or winter forcing indoors.

CULTIVARS: 'Carnegie' has white flowers. 'Delft Blue' produces pale blue blooms.

RETICULATED IRIS

Reticulated irises return year after year to grace your garden with their delicate spring flowers. Tuck them into beds, borders, and rock gardens; they look great in pots, too.

DESCRIPTION: Reticulated irises grow from small bulbs. The dainty blue, purple, or white, early spring flowers have three upright petals (known as standards) and three outward-arching petals (known as falls). The falls have gold and/or white markings. The grass-like, dark green leaves are short at bloom time but elongate after the flowers fade; they ripen and die back to the ground by early summer.

HEIGHT AND SPREAD: Height of flowers 4–6 inches (10–15 cm); leaves to about 12 inches (30 cm) tall. Spread to 2 inches (5 cm).

BEST SITE AND CLIMATE: Full sun; average, well-drained soil. Zones 5–9.

GROWING GUIDELINES: Plant the bulbs in fall. Set them in individual holes or larger planting areas dug 3–4 inches (7.5–10 cm) deep. For propagation, lift and divide clumps after the leaves turn yellow.

LANDSCAPE USES: The delicate, lightly fragrant blooms are beautiful in spring beds and borders. For extra color, combine them with Grecian windflowers (*Anemone blanda*) and early crocus. Reticulated irises also grow well in pots for spring bloom outdoors or winter forcing indoors.

CULTIVARS: 'Cantab' is pale blue with orange-marked falls. 'Clairette' has sky blue standards and deep blue falls marked with white. 'Harmony' is medium blue with gold markings. 'Natascha' has white flowers with yellow-striped falls.

| *Leucojum aestivum* | Amaryllidaceae | *Lilium* hybrids | Liliaceae |

SUMMER SNOWFLAKE

LILIES

Despite their name, summer snowflakes actually bloom in spring. Plant the small bulbs in groups; over time, they'll form large clumps.

Lilies are excellent as cut flowers; pick them when the first one or two buds open. You may want to remove the orange anthers to keep them from dropping pollen on furniture.

OTHER COMMON NAMES: Giant snowflake.

DESCRIPTION: Clumps of strap-shaped, green leaves emerge in early spring. In mid- to late-spring, plants produce slender, green flowering stems tipped with loose clusters of nodding, bell-shaped, ¾-inch (18 mm) wide flowers. The white flowers have a green spot near the tip of each petal. After bloom, the leaves turn yellow and die back to the ground by midsummer.

HEIGHT AND SPREAD: Height of foliage and flowers to 18 inches (30 cm); spread to 6 inches (15 cm).

BEST SITE AND CLIMATE: Full sun to partial shade; moist but well-drained soil with added organic matter. Zones 4–9.

GROWING GUIDELINES: In early fall, set bulbs in individual holes or larger planting areas dug 4 inches (10 cm) deep. Space them about 6 inches (15 cm) apart. For propagation, divide in early fall.

LANDSCAPE USES: Grow them with tulips and daffodils in flower beds and borders. Interplant with summer- and fall-blooming annuals that will fill in when the bulbs go dormant. Summer snowflakes also look great naturalized in moist meadows and woodlands.

OTHER SPECIES:

L. vernum, spring snowflake, blooms in early spring and has single, white, green-marked flowers on 6–8-inch (15–20 cm) tall stems. Zones 5–9.

DESCRIPTION: Lilies grow from scaly bulbs. They produce upright, unbranched stems with narrow to lance-shaped, green leaves in spring through early summer. By early to late summer (depending on the hybrid), the long, plump flower buds open to showy, flat or funnel-shaped flowers. After bloom, the leaves and stems usually stay green until late summer or early fall.

HEIGHT AND SPREAD: Height 2–5 feet (60–150 cm), depending on the hybrid; spread usually 6–12 inches (15–30 cm).

BEST SITE AND CLIMATE: Full sun to partial shade; average, well-drained soil. Usually Zones 4–8.

GROWING GUIDELINES: Handle the scaly bulbs gently, planting them in fall or early spring, as soon as they are available. If you plan to plant in spring, it's smart to prepare the planting area in fall and cover it with a thick mulch so it will be ready when your bulbs arrive. Dig individual holes or larger planting areas 6–8 inches (15–20 cm) deep, and loosen the soil in the bottom. After carefully filling in around the bulbs, water to settle the soil. Mulch to keep the bulbs cool and moist. Water during dry spells, especially before flowering. Pinch off spent flowers where they join the stem. Cut stems to the ground when the leaves turn yellow; divide clumps at the same time only if needed for propagation.

LILIES—CONTINUED   ## MAGIC LILY

Lilies have upright, outward-facing, or nodding blooms in white and shades of pink, red, orange, yellow, and lavender; some are streaked or shaded with other colors.

Magic lily bulbs produce leaves in spring and leafless flower stalks in late summer. Some gardeners like to combine them with bushy plants to hide the bare stems.

LANDSCAPE USES: Lilies add height and color to any flower bed or border. They're also elegant mixed into foundation plantings, grouped with shrubs, or naturalized in woodlands. Combine them with mounding annuals, perennials, or groundcovers that can shade the soil and keep the bulbs cool.

HYBRIDS: Asiatic hybrids bloom in early summer in a range of bright and pastel colors. The 4–6-inch (10–15 cm) wide flowers are usually upward facing but can also be outward facing or nodding. They bloom atop sturdy stems usually 24–36 inches (60–90 cm) tall. 'Enchantment' is a dependable cultivar with glowing red-orange flowers.

Aurelian hybrids bloom in midsummer and have large trumpet-shaped, bowl-shaped, nodding, or starry flowers on 4–6-foot (1.2–1.8 m) tall stems. The 6–8 inch (15–20 cm) wide flowers come in a wide range of colors and are usually fragrant. 'Black Dragon' has large, trumpet-shaped blooms that are white on the inside and maroon on the outside.

Oriental hybrids bloom in late summer and have large flowers in crimson red, pink, white, or white with yellow stripes; many blooms are spotted with pink or red. The richly fragrant flowers grow to 10 inches (25 cm) long and may be bowl-shaped or flat-faced; some have petals with recurved tips. 'Stargazer' has cherry red, white-edged blooms on 3-foot (90 cm) tall stems.

DESCRIPTION: Slender, greenish brown, leafless stems rise from the ground in late summer to early fall. They are topped with loose clusters of funnel-shaped, rosy pink flowers up to 4 inches (10 cm) long. The broad, strap-shaped, green leaves usually begin to emerge several weeks after the blooms fade. The foliage elongates in spring and dies back to the ground in summer, 1–2 months before new blooms appear.

HEIGHT AND SPREAD: Height of flowers to 24 inches (60 cm); leaves to 12 inches (30 cm). Spread to 6 inches (15 cm).

BEST SITE AND CLIMATE: Full sun to partial shade; average, well-drained soil that's dry in summer. Zones 5–9.

GROWING GUIDELINES: Plant bulbs as soon as they are available in midsummer. Set them in individual holes or larger planting areas dug 4–5 inches (10–12.5 cm) deep. Space bulbs about 8 inches (20 cm) apart. Water during dry spells in fall and spring. Protect the leaves over winter with a loose mulch, such as evergreen branches, pine needles, or straw. For propagation, divide bulbs in early- to mid-summer, as soon as the leaves have died; otherwise, leave the bulbs undisturbed to form large clumps.

LANDSCAPE USES: They grow best when naturalized on slopes, in groundcovers, or in low-maintenance areas.

Muscari armeniacum   Liliaceae

GRAPE HYACINTH

Once planted, grape hyacinths are trouble-free. They natural-
ize well under trees and shrubs, and they look quite attractive
combined with groundcovers.

DESCRIPTION: Grape hyacinths grow from small bulbs.
The narrow, grass-like, green leaves appear in fall
and elongate through the spring. The clumps are
accented by short, leafless stems topped with dense
spikes of grape-like blooms in early spring. The
individual purple-blue, white-rimmed flowers are
only ¼ inch (6 mm) wide. The leaves turn yellow
and die back to the ground by early summer.

HEIGHT AND SPREAD: Height of flowers and foliage 6–8 inches (15–20 cm); spread 3–4 inches
(7.5–10 cm).

BEST SITE AND CLIMATE: Full sun to partial shade
(under deciduous trees and shrubs); average, well-
drained soil. Zones 4–8.

GROWING GUIDELINES: Plant bulbs in early- to mid-
fall, as soon as they are available. Set them in
individual holes or larger planting areas dug 2–3
inches (5–7.5 cm) deep. Space the bulbs about
4 inches (10 cm) apart. For propagation, divide just
after the leaves die back in early summer. Otherwise, leave the bulbs undisturbed to form sweeps
of spring color.

LANDSCAPE USES: Scatter the bulbs liberally throughout flower beds and borders. Mix them with primroses, pansies, daffodils, and tulips for an unforgettable spring show. You can also grow them in
containers for outdoor bloom in spring or indoor
forcing in winter.

Narcissus hybrids   Amaryllidaceae

DAFFODILS

It's hard to imagine a garden without at least a few daffodils
for spring color. Grow them in borders, plant them under trees,
or naturalize them in low-maintenance areas.

DESCRIPTION: Daffodils grow from large, pointed
bulbs. Clumps of flat, strap-shaped, green leaves
emerge in early spring, along with leafless flower
stalks. Depending on the cultivar, the sometimes-
fragrant flowers appear in early-, mid-, or late-
spring. Each flower has a cup or trumpet (technically known as a corona) and an outer ring
of petals (known as the perianth). The single or
double blooms are most commonly white or yellow
but may also have pink, green, or orange parts or
markings. The leaves usually remain green until
midsummer, at which time they turn yellow and
die back to the ground.

HEIGHT AND SPREAD: Height of foliage and flowers
6–20 inches (15–50 cm), depending on the cultivar;
spread usually 4–8 inches (10–20 cm).

BEST SITE AND CLIMATE: Full sun to partial shade;
average, well-drained soil with added organic
matter. Zones 4–8.

GROWING GUIDELINES: Plant the bulbs in early- to
mid-fall. Set them in individual holes or larger
planting areas dug 4–8 inches (10–20 cm) deep.
(Use the shallower depth for smaller bulbs; plant
large bulbs deeply to discourage bulbs from splitting and to promote larger flowers.) Space small
types 3–4 inches (7.5–10 cm) apart and large types
8–10 inches (20–25 cm) apart. Top-dress the
planted bulbs with compost in early spring. Pinch

DAFFODILS—Continued

SIBERIAN SQUILL

Established daffodil clumps can live for years with little or no care; these dependable bulbs are seldom bothered by insects, diseases, or animal pests.

The deep blue blooms of Siberian squill look marvelous in masses. They also combine beautifully with other spring-flowering bulbs, annuals, and perennials.

off developing seed capsules. Allow the leaves to turn yellow before cutting them back or pulling them out; braiding or bundling the leaves with rubber bands can interfere with ripening and weaken bulbs. For propagation, divide clumps after the leaves die back.

LANDSCAPE USES: Create unforgettable combinations by grouping daffodils with other early bloomers, including pansies, crocus, Siberian squill (*Scilla sibirica*), grape hyacinths (*Muscari* spp.), and Grecian windflower (*Anemone blanda*). Daffodils grow especially well with groundcovers, such as Japanese pachysandra (*Pachysandra terminalis*) and common periwinkle (*Vinca minor*), which can mask the ripening leaves. Grow some daffodils in containers for spring bloom outdoors or winter forcing indoors. And don't forget to include some in the cutting garden for spring arrangements! The cut stems release a thick sap that can harm other flowers, so collect daffodils separately and let the stems sit in cool water overnight before mixing them with other blooms in arrangements.

CULTIVARS: In catalogs, daffodils are often listed under different divisions, based on their flower forms. Check the photographs and plant descriptions to find the colors, shapes, and sizes you like best.

DESCRIPTION: Siberian squills grow from small bulbs. They produce narrow, strap-shaped, green leaves and leafless flower stems starting in late winter. By early- to mid-spring, the flower stems are topped with clusters of nodding, starry or bell-shaped blue flowers to ½ inch (12 mm) across. By early summer, the leaves gradually turn yellow and die back to the ground.

HEIGHT AND SPREAD: Height of flowers and foliage to 6 inches (15 cm). Spread 2–3 inches (5–7.5 cm).

BEST SITE AND CLIMATE: Full sun to partial shade; average, well-drained soil. Zones 3–8.

GROWING GUIDELINES: Plant bulbs in early- to mid-fall, as soon as they are available. Set them in individual holes or larger planting areas dug 3–4 inches (7.5–10 cm) deep. Established bulbs are trouble-free. For propagation, divide bulbs after the leaves turn yellow; otherwise, leave them undisturbed to spread into large clumps.

LANDSCAPE USES: Tuck them into beds and borders with pansies, primroses, and daffodils. They are also excellent for naturalizing in lawns and low-maintenance areas and under trees and shrubs; just wait until the bulb leaves have turned yellow to mow. Siberian squills also grow well in containers for spring bloom outdoors or winter forcing indoors.

CULTIVARS: 'Alba' has white flowers. 'Spring Beauty' is a popular cultivar that has deep purple-blue flowers.

TULIPS

Hybrid tulips often bloom poorly after the first year. For a great show each year, pull them out after bloom and replace them with summer annuals; plant new tulips in fall.

Tulips bloom in practically every color, including white and near black; some are also attractively striped, marked, or shaded with two or more colors.

DESCRIPTION: Tulips grow from plump, pointed bulbs. The bulbs produce broad, dusty-green leaves that are sometimes striped with maroon in early- to mid-spring. The slender, upright, usually unbranched flower stems are topped with showy single or double flowers up to 4 inches (10 cm) across. By midsummer, leaves gradually turn yellow and die back to the ground.

HEIGHT AND SPREAD: Height from 6–30 inches (15–90 cm), depending on the cultivar; spread 6–10 inches (15–25 cm).

BEST SITE AND CLIMATE: Full sun to partial shade; average, well-drained soil that's dry in summer. Usually best in Zones 3–8; in Zones 9 and 10, treat hybrid tulips as annuals and plant precooled bulbs each year in late fall or early winter.

GROWING GUIDELINES: Plant bulbs in mid- to late-fall. Set them in individual holes or larger planting areas dug 4–6 inches (10–15 cm) deep. (If possible, planting 8 inches (20 cm) deep is even better, since it can discourage bulbs from splitting and in turn promote better flowering in following years.) Space bulbs about 6 inches (15 cm) apart. Pinch off the developing seedpods after flowering, and allow the leaves to yellow before removing them. Or treat the hybrids like annuals and pull them out after bloom.

LANDSCAPE USES: Tulips' stately, colorful flowers are an indispensable part of the spring garden. In flower beds and borders, grow them with daffodils, pansies, primroses, bleeding hearts (*Dicentra* spp.), grape hyacinths (*Muscari* spp.), and forget-me-nots (*Myosotis* spp.). Tulips are also charming as cut flowers; pick them when the flowers are fully colored but still in bud. You can also grow tulips in containers and force them for winter bloom indoors.

CULTIVARS: In catalogs, hybrid tulips are often listed under different divisions, based on their flower forms and bloom times. Look at the photographs and check the descriptions to find the colors, heights, and bloom times that will work best in your garden. 'Angelique' has ruffled, petal-packed, double, pale pink flowers on 16-inch (40 cm) tall stems. 'Apricot Beauty' has beautiful peach-colored blooms on 14-inch (35 cm) tall stems. 'Ballade' grows to 24 inches (60 cm) tall and has reddish purple, white-edged, pointed petals that arch outward. 'Maureen' reaches 30 inches (90 cm) tall and has white flowers. 'Mrs. J. T. Scheepers' has sunny yellow blooms on 30-inch (90 cm) tall stems. 'Negrita' grows to 16 inches (40 cm) tall and has purple flowers. 'Queen of the Night' has dark maroon-black blooms on 24-inch (60 cm) tall stems. 'Red Emperor' grows to 18 inches (45 cm) tall and has large, scarlet flowers. 'Red Riding Hood' has black-centered red flowers and purple-striped leaves on 8-inch (20 cm) tall stems.

USDA Plant
Hardiness Zone Map

The map that follows shows the United States and Canada divided into 10 zones. Each zone is based on a 10°F (5.6°C) difference in average annual minimum temperature. Some areas are considered too high in elevation for plant cultivation and so are not assigned to any zone. There are also island zones that are warmer or cooler than surrounding areas because of differences in elevation; they have been given a zone different from the surrounding areas. Many large urban areas are in a warmer zone than the surrounding land.

Plants grow best within an optimum range of temperatures. The range may be wide for some species and narrow for others. Plants also differ in their ability to survive frost and in their sun or shade requirements.

The zone ratings indicate conditions where designated plants will grow well and not merely survive. Refer to the map to find out which zone you are in. In the plant by plant guides, you'll find recommendations for the plants that grow best in your zone.

Many plants may survive in zones warmer or colder than their recommended zone range. Remember that other factors, including wind, soil type, soil moisture and drainage capability, humidity, snow, and winter sunshine, may have a great effect on growth.

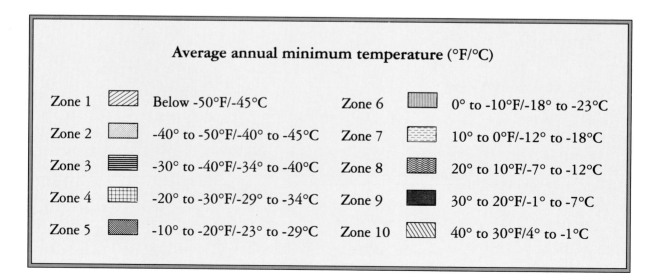

Average annual minimum temperature (°F/°C)

Zone 1	Below -50°F/-45°C	Zone 6	0° to -10°F/-18° to -23°C
Zone 2	-40° to -50°F/-40° to -45°C	Zone 7	10° to 0°F/-12° to -18°C
Zone 3	-30° to -40°F/-34° to -40°C	Zone 8	20° to 10°F/-7° to -12°C
Zone 4	-20° to -30°F/-29° to -34°C	Zone 9	30° to 20°F/-1° to -7°C
Zone 5	-10° to -20°F/-23° to -29°C	Zone 10	40° to 30°F/4° to -1°C

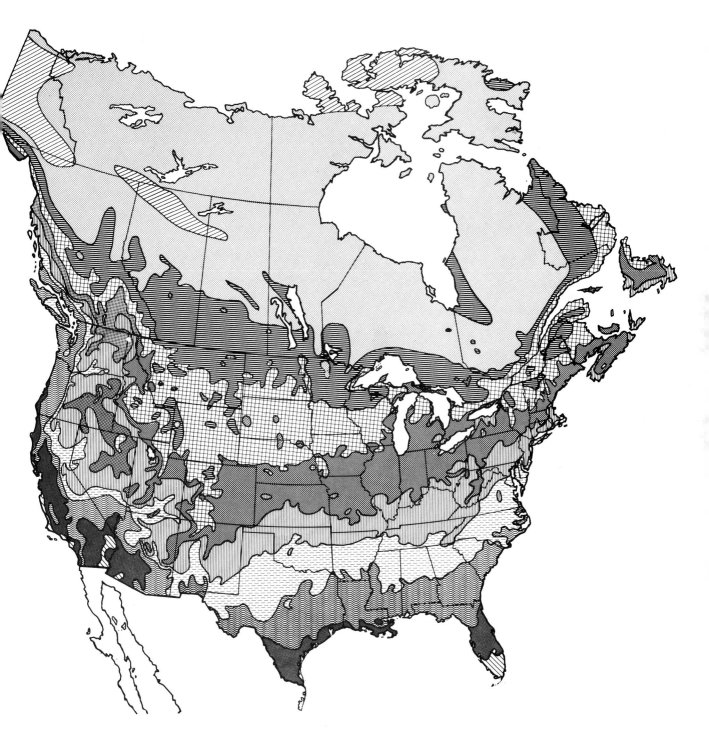

ACKNOWLEDGMENTS

Photo Credits

Heather Angel: page 130 (bottom).

A–Z Botanical Collection: photographer Elsa M. Megson: page 139 (left); photographer Bjorn Svensson: page 18 (bottom right).

Gillian Beckett: pages 60 (right), 76 (left), 78 (left), 80 (right), 86 (right), 91 (right), 92 (left), 95 (left), and 144 (left).

Bruce Coleman Limited: photographer Eric Crichton: page 51; photographer Hans Reinhard: half title page and page 128 (left).

Thomas Eltzroth: pages 55 (bottom), 58, 59 (right), 60 (left), 61 (left and right), 63 (left), 64 (left), 65 (left and right), 66 (left and right), 68 (right), 69 (right), 70 (right), 71 (left and right), 72 (left), 74 (left and right), 75 (left and right), 76 (right), 77 (left), 78 (right), 79 (right), 80 (left), 82 (left), 84 (left and right), 86 (left), 88 (left and right), 90 (left), 91 (left), 93 (left and right), 94 (left), 95 (right), 96 (right), 97 (left), 99 (left), 100 (left and right), 101 (left), 102 (right), 103 (left and right), 140 (right), 142 (left), 146 (left), and 149 (left).

Derek Fell: pages 18 (bottom left), 35 (top), 38, 41 (left), 81 (right), 106 (top left), 129 (right), and 150 (right).

The Garden Picture Library: photographer Lynne Brotchie: pages 26 (bottom right), 30 (bottom), 39 (bottom left), and 83 (right); photographer Rex Butcher: page 21 (right); photographer Brian Carter: page 40 (top), 123 (bottom), and 147 (left); photographer Christopher Gallagher: 39 (bottom right); photographer John Glover: pages 27 (bottom), 34 (left), 54 (left), and 89 (right); photographer S. Harte: page 12; photographer Neil Holmes: page 23; photographer Michael Howes: pages 44 and 132 (bottom); photographer Lamontagne: endpapers, pages 45 (left), 47, 52, 56 (left), 67 (left), 128 (right), 135, and 140 (left); photographer Jane Legate: pages 133 (bottom) and 136 (bottom); photographer Zara McCalmont: pages 49 (top), 110 (bottom), and 117 (top left); photographers Mayer/Le Scanff: pages 48, 114 (top), and 126 (bottom right); photographer Jerry Pavia: page 34 (right); photographer Gary Rogers: page 35 (bottom); photographer J. S. Sira: back cover (bottom) and page 126 (top right); photographer Steven Wooster: page 123 (top left).

Holt Studios International: photographer Nigel Cattlin: pages 56 (right), 90 (right), and 133 (top).

Andrew Lawson: pages 7 (bottom left), 24 (top), 40 (bottom), 41 (right), 42, 108 (bottom right), and 134 (top left).

S & O Mathews: back cover (top), opposite contents page, pages 11 (right), 14 (top right), 15, 16 (top), 20 (top), 24 (bottom), 25 (right), 26 (bottom left), 30 (top left), 32, 33 (bottom), 36 (right), 37 (right), 50, 53 (top right and bottom), 59 (left), 62 (right), 63 (right), 69 (left), 83 (left), 97 (right), 98 (left and right), 107 (top and bottom), 108 (bottom left), 111 (left), 112 (top), 113 (top right, bottom left, and bottom right), 117 (bottom right), 122 (top and bottom right), 124, 126 (bottom left), 137, 139 (right), 143 (left and right), 145 (left), 147 (right), 149 (right), 151 (right), 152 (left), and 153 (right).

Clive Nichols: back cover (center), opposite title page, copyright page, pages 7 (top left), 8, 11 (left), 16 (bottom), 17 (left and right), 19, 22, 25 (left), 26 (top), 27 (top), 28, 30 (top right), 31, 33 (top left and top right), 36 (left), 37 (left), 54 (right), 67 (right), 104, 106 (top right and bottom), 109, 110 (top), 111 (right), 112 (bottom), 113 (top left), 116 (left and right), 117 (top right and bottom left), 118 (left and right), 119 (left and right), 120 (left), 122 (bottom left), 123 (top right), 126 (top left), 127 (top, bottom left, and bottom right), 130 (top left and top right), 131 (right), 132 (top left), 134 (top right), 136 (top), 142 (right), 145 (right), 146 (right), 148 (right), and 151 (left).

Jerry Pavia: pages 39 (top), 68 (left), 72 (right), 73 (left and right), 79 (left), 81 (left), 89 (left), 96 (left), 102 (left), 144 (right), 148 (left), 150 (left), and 153 (left).

Joanne Pavia: pages 82 (right) and 108 (top).

Photos Horticultural: front cover, title page, pages 18 (top), 20 (bottom), 21 (left), 45 (center and right), 46, 49 (bottom left, bottom center, and bottom right), 53 (top left), 55 (top), 64 (right), 87 (right), 114 (bottom), 115 (left and right), 120 (right), 129 (left), 131 (left), 132 (top right), 134 (bottom), and 152 (right).

Harry Smith Collection: pages 62 (left), 70 (left), 85 (left and right), 87 (left), 92 (right), 94 (right), 99 (right), 138, and 141 (left and right).

Weldon Russell: pages 7 (bottom right), 77 (right), and 101 (right).